CENTENNIAL COMMEMORATIVE
ISSUE
1873   1973

THIS BOOK and its companion
pure silver Coin-medal are issued
to commemorate the 100th Anniversary
of the Mescalero Apache Reservation

_____

May 29, 1973

And is limited to 15,000 copies
No. **LIBRARY**

Photograph by Indian Tribal Series

SIERRA BLANCA, one of the peaks sacred to the Mescalero people, seen under its frequent spring cloud cover from the new road to the Cieneguita recreation area now being developed.

THE
MESCALERO
APACHE
PEOPLE

by Henry F. Dobyns

Scientific Editors: Henry F. Dobyns and Robert C. Euler
General Editor: John I. Griffin

PUBLISHED BY INDIAN TRIBAL SERIES / PHOENIX

PRESIDENT WENDELL CHINO of the Mescalero Apache Tribe in his office at Mescalero, New Mexico.

W HEN FRANCISCO VÁZQUEZ DE CORONADO led his Spanish cavalry onto the Great Plains in 1540, he found there a highly mobile population of bison hunters. They very probably included southern Athapascan-speaking ancestors of the present Mescalero Apache people.

The Spaniards described the early Plains Apaches from whom the contemporary Mescaleros descend as hunters and food gatherers who utilized dogs to transport their goods. Even then, they undoubtedly roasted many *agave* hearts in earth ovens, dried the product, and stored it in hand-woven baskets or skin bags. That economic pursuit later would lead Spaniards to label them "Mescaleros" from the Spanish term "mescal" for the *agave* plant and the suffix "ero" meaning "person who makes."

The abundant bison of the Great Plains provided ancestral Mescaleros with intestines to

1

clean and loop over their shoulders for canteens, and with skins from which to fashion their clothing, caps, and their housing. They inhabited *tipis,* a very portable kind of home. Slender but stout poles provided a framework over which to spread hides. When moving camp, the people employed their tipi poles to make dog *travois* — one end tied to the dog's burden-harness, and the other skidding and bouncing along the ground. They trained their dogs to howl for help when loads fell into disarray. The tanned bison hides women spread over the tipi pole frame to form a warm house moved on the dog travois, along with other household goods. Mothers themselves probably carried the wooden cradle — boards padded with soft skins to which infants were strapped.

Ancestral Mescalero men hunted bison with bow and arrow, probably with the aid of their dogs. Each man made his own weapons, which included slings, darts, and rope dart-throwers. They skinned their kills with a finger-sized stone blade hafted to a wooden handle. They sharpened it with their teeth! Their bison hunts followed a seasonal pattern. The entire population congregated in one large group in the fall for a bison hunt that extended through the winter. This physically arduous life produced what might be termed a "muscle culture." Parents taught their children to develop their strength, fortitude and endurance from the

2

Photograph by H. F. Robinson, Courtesy Museum of New Mexico
A MESCALERO APACHE WOMAN and her baby firmly strapped in a cradleboard
beside their wickiup in 1906. Mescalero women carried their infants on such
cradleboards from prehistoric times.

earliest possible moment. Such games as the children might play mostly prepared them for a strenuous life.

In view of the tenacity with which the Mescaleros later clung to the agricultural portion of their annual cycle, one must conclude that they were enthusiastic maize, bean and squash and probably gourd growers in 1540. In the spring, the people scattered out in small groups to take advantage of easily cultivated fertile spots where they could plant their crops and anticipate good harvests.

Plains Apache society had probably already developed an internal social structure that continues to the present day. Ancestral Mescaleros reckoned descent through women, a custom fostering residence by men in their wives' households. Mothers and daughters were inseparable, constantly cooperating to collect wild foods, to prepare and cook them. The matriarch's husband, unmarried sons and sons-in-law all brought their game to her cooking fire. Each wife carried part of the prepared food home to eat with her spouse and children. For ancestral Mescaleros so strongly tabooed sexual relations between a man and his wife's mother that the poor fellow was required to avoid interpersonal interaction with her at all! Thus, the very sentiments that made for a strong family through the generations in terms of alliances between related women also fostered brittle

4

marital unions, and encouraged the social dispersal of the Mescalero people during the agricultural season into minimum nuclear family farming units. A superlatively skilled hunter might marry sisters, each of whom erected her own tipi.

Local groups of parents, their unmarried children, and their married daughters with their husbands and children frequently traveled together. Each group based itself on a landmark whose name provided a name for the group. Neighboring local groups formed defensive-offensive bands.

Living in local groups composed of relatives, ancestral Mescaleros addressed one another with kinship terms. Parents called their offspring "son" or "daughter" and they spoke in turn to "father" and "mother." In all other cases, relatives employed a reciprocal term. Grandparents, for example, addressed their grandchildren by the same term the latter used to speak to them. A single term lumped all brothers and sisters of one's mother or father. Men used the same term of address for their sisters and female cousins, but worked with the former and avoided the latter.

During prehistoric centuries of moving about on foot, Plains Apaches developed a pragmatic method for dealing with the problem that arose from time to time when a mother bore twin children. Recognizing the probability that both

5

would die should their mother attempt to rear both — because the mother who spent half the year walking and running rapidly from camp to camp as the tribe hunted grazing bison could efficiently care for only one — ancestral Mescaleros killed one twin shortly after birth. Like virtually everything else, twin-killing had its religious justification and rationale, for Plains Apache life was thoroughly suffused with an aura of supernatural power, explained in many myths.

Although ancestral Mescaleros practiced this special form of infanticide, they lived in mortal fear of ghosts of the dead. Like other native Americans, they believed ghosts persecuted the living in the guise of an owl. They tried to scare owls away from their camps, for they heard warnings of impending death in the owl's hoot.

The main concern of ancestral Mescalero religion and its ceremonies was maintenance of an individual in good health. Given the sheer physical rigors of roaming hunts during half the year, with frequent accidents during trips between campsites, a constant anxiety over well-being among Mescaleros was very understandable! Contact with animals such as bears and snakes caused the gravest illnesses in the Mescalero view. Even in camp, a child could drown in the stream where people drank. The uncertainties of horticulture on the Great Plains with their droughts and floods, early and late

6

frosts, could have but added worries about food supplies. Small wonder that Plains Apaches prayed frequently, often offered food and sacred pollen to their gods, added stones to trailside shrine-cairns, performed rain-bringing ceremonies, and learned the food value of scores of wild plants to which they might turn when the harvest and hunt failed.

Small wonder also that the Plains Apaches should have developed trading relationships with the sedentary Pueblo farmers on the Río Grande and other streams in modern New Mexico. Never great hunters, and timid about encroaching upon the hunting ranges of the Apaches, who could fight fiercely if need be, the Puebloans were content to trade agricultural surplus for warm bison robes tanned by Plains hunters, who wintered after the fall-winter hunt near the Pueblos. Sun-dried bison meat also entered the Apache-Pueblo trade, and ancestral Mescaleros probably also traded dried roasted *agave* hearts to the sweet-hungry Pueblo dwellers. The Pueblo trade provided special treats during good years for the Plains people, and emergency agricultural food supplies during bad years.

Hard though life may have been on the Great Plains, the ancestral Mescalero people found time to fashion several musical instruments to play to accompany ritual chants. They made and played the musical bow, and both a tambourine type drum and a pottery drum.

The Plains Apaches paid little attention to passing Spanish exploring expeditions. After Spaniards settled among the Pueblo peoples along the Río Grande in 1598, on the other hand, ancestral Mescaleros began to pay a good deal of attention to them. Plains Apaches plainly discerned the potential to them of the horses Spanish settlers rode into the colonial Province of New Mexico.

Colonial records indicate that Plains Apache raids on New Mexican settlers intensified beginning around 1630, reaching peak intensity by 1660. The ancestral Mescaleros and other Plains Apaches had embarked upon their greatest cultural adventure and entered their most prosperous century. The Plains Apaches quickly mounted the horse, touching off an economic boom and geo-political explosion across the southern Great Plains.

As long as Plains Apaches followed bison on foot, they never could defeat in battle the more sedentary horticultural Indians on their borders. Aboriginal warriors fought battles by lining up in parallel formations, or dividing into two wings to engage. Thus, the larger force enjoyed a tremendous advantage in being able to outflank its foe. The horticultural tribes east of the Plains Apaches grew enough food to support large village populations and joined in loose war confederations giving them battle superiority.

When Plains Apaches acquired horses, they quickly won military supremacy over unmounted tribes. They abandoned infantry for cavalry tactics. They learned to fire their short bow from horseback. They tipped long lances with Spanish saber blades and wielded them from the firm seat of a Spanish style leather-covered high-cantled saddle, guiding their war horses with Spanish metal bits, while thrusting their toes into metal stirrups. Ancestral Mescaleros carried Spanish style shields and wore leather body armor into battle. Whether they preferred the red, green, blue or white body-armor paint recorded for Plains Apache cavalrymen of the 17th Century is not certain. They also armored their war-steeds with buffalo hides with sand glued to the surface.

Such armor effectively protected ancestral Mescaleros against the arrow although it offered no protection against bullets. Thus, the body-armored Apaches riding armored war-horses achieved nearly as great a military superiority over unarmored native American infantrymen as Spaniards had themselves. They lacked only firearms to achieve military parity with Spaniards, and their metal-tipped cavalry lances provided penetrating power to dispatch even armored infantry.

Consequently Plains Apaches greatly and

rapidly expanded their territory during the 17th Century as they acquired horses and mastered cavalry warfare. Territorial expansion brought many material benefits. Plains Apaches had larger hunting ranges in which to pursue bison on horseback, as well as antelope, elk, deer and other game. They enjoyed access to more stands of *agave* (or "Century plant") for roasting mescal, as well as thickets of fruit and nut bearing shrubs and trees, and meadows of seed-yielding grasses and other plants. Most of all, expansion made available numerous fertile, easily cultivated river-bottom horticultural fields.

Plains Apache territorial aggression also opened tremendous expanses of natural pasture to feed growing horse herds. As an animal that could do everything the prehistoric dog could for the ancestral Mescaleros, the horse allowed an expansion of everything that depended on animal transport. The larger-stronger horse could pull tipi poles longer and heavier than those any dog could. The horse could also haul a heavier load of the tanned bison skins matrons used to cover taller tipi frameworks. Moreover, horses provided hunters with increased range in searching out herds and greatly augmented speed in hunting. Thus, the horse enabled hunters to kill more bison to provide additional hides to tan to cover enlarged tipi frames.

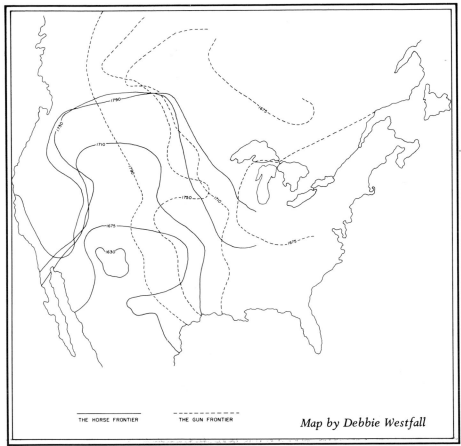

THE HORSE FRONTIER   THE GUN FRONTIER   *Map by Debbie Westfall*

MAP 1. The diffusion of horses among Great Plains tribes in North America from 1630 to 1790, related to westward expansion of French and British trade areas that supplied Indians with firearms during the same period. Plains Apaches defeated and ousted other native Americans from central Texas, eastern New Mexico and Colorado, central and western Oklahoma, Kansas and western Nebraska between about 1620 and 1725.

A larger kill meant more animal protein in the Mescalero diet, and probably increased fertility because food supply improved relative to energy expended. Moreover, hard on pregnant women as horseback riding may have been, it was not as difficult for them as hiking all over the southern Great Plains on foot carrying babies and household gear. Pregnant women could even ride a horse-travois, if need be, as well as tie infants' cradleboards to them. Consequently, the Mescalero people began to increase in numbers in the second third of the 17th Century. The improved hunting capability horses brought also improved clothing. A plentiful hide supply allowed women to tan and tailor more clothes, which the horse travois could now transport. Almost surely the enlarged territory also contained more eagle nests to raid for eaglets to rear in captivity for their feathers for ceremonial use.

During this period, the people quite likely continued the laborious tasks of preparing mescal more because they relished its tangy sweetness than because they needed its nourishment. To enjoy this dish, women had to cooperate in groups large enough to work rapidly. First, they found stout sticks and fashioned one end into a blade to drive through the plant's root by pounding the other end with a stone. Prosperity brought metal knives from the Spaniards to accelerate trimming the spiny leaf-ends from the heart. Digging a pit oven still meant plenty of hard, grubby work, however, followed by the task of carrying heavy rocks to line it. Spanish axes and hatchets facilitated felling trees for the hot fire to heat the stones so the trimmed *agave* hearts could be piled in the hot oven, covered with damp leaves and earth. A night or two later, the cooks opened the pit and the group feasted. After everyone ate all he or she wanted of the warm, sweet mass — or all a person thought he should consume in view of the laxative effect of the mescal — the surplus was spread on flat stones to dry. Later, women transported dried mescal to caches to store. Later, Mescaleros could break off chunks to chew, spitting out the tough fibers after extracting the last bit of sugar and flavor. Or, they could trade dried mescal to Pueblo Indians for bits of Spanish metal, or maize and beans.

Plains Apache traders acquired very valuable new trade-goods during the century of prosperity. With horses, ancestral Mescalero warriors overwhelmed unmounted tribesmen on the frontiers, taking many captives. Some comely young women the warriors kept as concubines or even wives, somewhat weakening the social dominance of Mescalero matriarchs, but hardly increasing the durability of marriages. Knowing that New Mexican Spaniards also coveted such slaves as household servants and others to sell to the textile factories of New Spain, the warriors deliberately took most captives to the Spanish

MESCALERO APACHE TIPIS and tipi frame. This encampment was photographed in 1906, and shows reservation mountain environment. Nonetheless, the tipi poles are still arranged as they were

Photograph by H. F. Robinson, Courtesy Museum of New Mexico
centuries before on the Great Plains as soon as horses made possible transporting poles of such length. Brush shades of the type visible behind the tipi framework on the left often supplemented tipis.

settlements for sale. Such prisoners served the Plains Apaches well in lieu of cash with which to purchase Spanish metals and mounts.

During the 17th Century, Plains Apaches apparently built up a new level of social organization based on the horse. Quite possibly ancestral Mescaleros followed hunting chiefs on semi-annual bison hunts when dogs carried most burdens. When horses increased the hunter's range, allowing larger hunting parties to work together, leadership emerged on a larger scale. Assembling these large hunting bands also facilitated massing cavalrymen to assault neighboring tribes in sufficient numbers to overwhelm the massed infantry of the horticulturalists along the eastern margin of the Great Plains. Consequently, chiefs of raiding bands appear to have become subject to the authority of a supreme war chief.

The century of Plains Apache prosperity saw the emergence, in all likelihood, of the Mescalero Apache people as a social and political entity — a tribe in the political sense. Led by a supreme war chief, they conquered an extensive territory which they controlled and exploited for a number of decades. They grew crops in it with their aboriginal horticultural technology. They hunted bison and other big game animals with the horse and metal-pointed arrows for their short-bows. They fought as cavalry on a Spanish model. They continued worrying about their

16

health. Curers continued to see visions convey-
ing supernatural power to them. Husbands continued to avoid their mothers-in-law, and wives
continued to prefer living near their mothers.

HALF A CENTURY OF CULTURAL
ADJUSTMENT 1725-1775

The seeds of ancestral Mescalero downfall lay
in the very success during the prosperous
century after 1630. Eventually, tribes beyond
the Apache borders managed to steal a few
horses, fashion their own lances, body armor
and horse caparisons equal to those Mescaleros
employed. Most serious of all, however, was the
acquisition of horses by northerly native Americans who lacked a strong economic and senti-
mental attachment to horticulture. Comanches
moved onto the Great Plains from northern
Plateau areas where the aboriginal population
grew no food. Whatever food Utes may once
have grown, they abandoned gardening for the
bison chase with great gusto. While some
mounted Utes reinforced the Hopis to resist
Spanish reconquest in 1692, these Indians began
stealing horses from New Mexicans in earnest
about 1704. By 1719, the Utes and their new
Comanche allies both clearly had passed through
the cultural transformation from infantry fighting to cavalry warfare. As non-farmers, both
tribes devoted themselves to hunting and raiding
the year round.

17

This provided them with a distinct military advantage over Plains Apaches. Comanches quickly learned where the horticultural Apaches cultivated summer crops. They could be certain of finding ancestral Mescaleros spread out over their vast territory in small matrilineal family units, planting, tilling and harvesting their crops during the warm months. Operating as a unified military unit, the Comanches attacked Plains Apache horticultural settlements one by one. Thus, they enjoyed the twin advantages of surprise and numerical superiority.

By 1719, Utes and Comanches had nibbled away the Plains Apache northern frontier because of the effective military initiative they enjoyed during half the year. Moreover, French explorers had found routes into Indian country west of the Mississippi River for trading with native Americans during the 1690's. They swapped guns and munitions for animal pelts, tallow, dried meat and slaves. A few guns filtered out to tribes which the Plains Apaches had pushed into the drainages of western tributaries of the Mississippi, thus shifting the balance of power against ancestral Mescaleros and other beneficiaries of the prosperous Apache century.

Plains Apaches began to seek an alliance with the New Mexicans. The avidity with which British and French traders pushed guns upon eastern Indians made it already too late. In

1720, enemy Plains tribes wiped out a joint Spanish-Apache cavalry expedition at the North and South Platte River junction. That defeat marked the end of Apache military supremacy on the Great Plains. Yet ancestral Mescaleros and other Apaches attempted to defend their northern territory until 1727. By that time, military pressure from mounted Pawnee, Ute and Comanche with their French firearms forced the Plains Apaches to abandon the area north of the Arkansas River.

By perhaps 1740, the Comanches formed an alliance with the Caddoan-speaking tribes which the Plains Apaches had pushed eastward. Both enjoyed a brisk trade in guns, ammunition, hatchets, knives, pots, etc., in exchange for bison hides and meat, horses and mules stolen from Plains Apaches and Spaniards, and Apache captives.

The Mescaleros, on the other hand, were plunged into immediate poverty when the military balance of power shifted between 1719 and 1727. They could no longer seize captives from Utes, Comanches, and Caddoans to sell as slaves to New Mexicans. Thus, they lost their most valuable trade goods. Bison hunting grounds rapidly diminished as they yielded territory to enemies, so they could take fewer hides, dry less meat for their own sustenance, much less to trade. At the same time, successful Ute and Comanche raids on their own horse herds and stores of metal for weapons and horse gear made them desperate to replace losses.

The Spaniards, accustomed to trading with friendly Plains Apaches for over a century, initially carried on in the usual manner. They encouraged refugee Plains Apaches to settle at Christian missions and take up a fully sedentary horticultural life. Mescaleros proved reluctant to abandon the rich rewards of bison hunting. They also recognized that Comanches located and attacked missions as easily as other horticultural settlements. The Spaniards attempted to protect Plains Apaches until an expedition under Texas Governor Diego Ortiz Parilla suffered decisive defeat on the Plains in 1759.

Thereafter, Plains Apaches faced a real survival crisis. Caught between the Comanche-Ute-Caddoan hammer and the Spanish frontier anvil, the Plains Apaches had to raid for horses and weaponry metal to replace their losses. They went to war with Spain. At the same time, forced out of the Great Plains, Mescaleros had to institute emergency research on the edibility of nuts, berries and other plant produce in a more arid environment. They had to learn to stalk deer in the New Mexican mountains, to build tipi frameworks of flexible, light poles so they could reach up to thatch them over with grass as the bison hide supply for tipi covers dwindled and disappeared through usage and destruction during enemy raids.

20

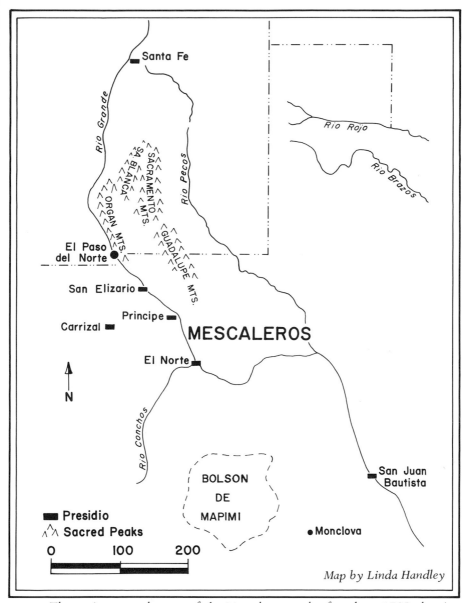

Santa Fe

Rio Grande

Rio Rojo

Rio Brazos

Rio Pecos

SACRAMENTO

SA BLANCA

MTS.

ORGAN MTS.

GUADALUPE MTS.

El Paso del Norte

San Elizario

Principe

Carrizal

MESCALEROS

El Norte

N

Rio Conchos

BOLSON

DE

MAPIMI

San Juan Bautista

Presidio

Sacred Peaks

Monclova

0   100   200

Map by Linda Handley

MAP 2. The environmental range of the Mescalero people after about 1725, showing the Spanish colonial frontier as of the 1770's. Mescaleros ranged east of the Rio Grande onto the Great Plains, north to Santa Fe, and south to the Bolson de Mapimi.

As the Mescaleros learned to survive in their new semi-arid territory, they had to learn to irrigate their crops. How soon they managed to do so remains uncertain. They may well have gone through half a century of very indifferent success at horticulture until later events brought them into direct contact with Indian irrigators whom they could emulate. Meanwhile, all the economic storms of a radically altered Mescalero condition in truth made them *mescaleros* of the highest order. The people survived, probably, on the *agave* plant above all other food resources. The *agave* yields its most delicious food in spring or early summer when a blossom stalk begins to shoot up from a mature plant, loaded with fruit sugar. Even before that, and in any season of necessity, one can eat the roasted *agave* heart and obtain a nutritious if not very sweet or palatable food. *Agave* was emergency food for desperate people, and the Mescaleros acquired their Spanish name during a truly desperate period of tribal emergency.

At the same time that Mescaleros turned to their old standby *agave* to survive, they learned to process mesquite bean-pods into *pinole* and to eat prickly pear cactus fruit and pinyon nuts. They also acquired such new cultural values as thirst-endurance in the semi-arid environment. They adapted the animal intestine canteen and skin containers of mobile life on the plains to desert survival.

As the Mescalero people suffered the hunger pangs of poverty, the chieftainship that emerged during the prosperous century strengthened in bands held together to protect members against a militarily superior enemy. As warriors fell in battle and as enemy attacks carried people off into slavery if not into death during enemy victory rituals, a strong Mescalero death fear deepened, and the quest for supernatural power spread widely. Nearly every person needed a supernatural guardian, "something to live by." Mescaleros came to fear more than ever that the success of a curer eventually depended upon his (or her) sacrificing, to avoid dying himself, the life of a near relative or friend whom he assisted and upon whom he relied. Year after year, people witnessed the death or capture of their dearest relatives, seemingly without rhyme or reason.

During the half century after the 1719-27 defeats, Mescalero women surely gained social and cultural importance. Men remained warriors, but did not succeed as in the past century of glory and male chauvinism, as they fought a rear-guard and often futile action. As hunters, men could not maintain the prosperity of bison-killing days in the more arid Southwest where new skills of stalking, surrounds, and drives had to be learned slowly, with great frustration. Women sustained the people with roasted *agave* hearts and new fruits, berries, nuts, seeds and

23

roots they learned to find and prepare. As female slaves and concubines Mescalero men brought into their homes during the prosperous century aged and died, they could not be replaced. Thus, Mescalero men found themselves newly dependent upon their own women for sexual gratification and sheer survival. What had surely been a happy homelife during the prosperous century turned increasingly bitter during the cultural adjustment to military inferiority, a new environment and poverty.

Yet this period of cultural shock probably enhanced Mescalero militarism. As military success became fleeting, women may have rewarded raiding success more overtly with food and sexual favors. High mortality rates made marriage partners invaluable. The Mescaleros probably strengthened the control of in-laws over remarriage of a widow or widower. Certainly in later times the family of a dead mate absolutely controlled the surviving spouse, often forcing a widower to marry a sister or cousin of his dead wife, or a widow to marry a brother or cousin of her dead husband. At the same time, women probably found easy rationalizations for stealing a cousin's spouse, and men for making off with a cousin's wife, a behavior pattern inconsistent with the kinship terminology.

The Mescaleros who had been Great Plainsmen par excellence, turned into premier mountaineers. As they retreated from native American

24

foes toward the Spanish frontier, they found mountain tops to be best-watered, best-wooded, most vegetated and most plentifully endowed with game in the semi-arid region. They learned to live at the relatively high altitudes of the mountain slopes and peaks. Whenever they learned to irrigate crops, Mescaleros found that the slopes, besides providing game and firewood and shelter, yielded precious water for irrigation.

HALF A CENTURY OF COLONIAL DEPENDENCY 1775-1825

[3] After the Spaniards began fighting the refugee Plains Apaches instead of trying to settle them in missions, they generally followed a no-quarter, no-peace policy. Here and there along the frontier, however, local military commanders succeeded in ignoring colonial policy and executed peace agreements with various Apache groups. Such was the situation at the royal Spanish fort at El Paso del Norte on the Río Grande. Rather than fight Mescaleros who occupied the area north of his post, the El Paso commandant executed a tentative peace agreement with Mescalero leaders in the 1760's, but was removed for so doing. Another attempt came in 1777.

These agreements were vital to the survival of the Mescalero people. Spanish allegiance would afford them one peaceful flank, where they might settle under the protective cannon of a Spanish post when need be to escape marauding Comanches. Moreover, peace might open up to them trade for metal to fashion into arrowpoints and other weapons and horse trappings, if not firearms. At the same time, they might remain free to hunt when Comanches and other hostile tribes were not on the immediate horizon.

On the other hand, a Spanish alliance would bring the Mescaleros face to face with another forced cultural adjustment. They would have to accommodate to a dependent relationship with arrogant colonial Spaniards. This involved learning a new language, wearing European-style clothing, consuming new foodstuffs such as wheat flour, and drinking alcoholic home-brew made from fermented sprouted maize kernels and distilled intoxicants of much greater power. Moreover, it meant serving the Spaniards of El Paso, Monclova and other posts as Indian scouts on campaigns against other Apaches, almost as soon as they first made peace, in order to convince the Spaniards that they should continue their Mescalero alliance.

Spanish pressures for Mescalero cultural change were not so great during the first years after their tentative peace agreement with the El Paso post commandant as they were after 1786. In that year, the Viceroy of New Spain, Bernardo de Gálvez, promulgated a new policy toward all Apaches. Compounded from his own

Photograph by Ben Wittick, Courtesy Museum of New Mexico

A MESCALERO APACHE WARRIOR, Ignacio, and his son about 1885. They wear a mixture of native Mescalero clothing — moccasins — and Spanish-Mexican apparel — vest, shirt, blanket, pants, powder horn.

experience in Louisiana and that of frontier commanders with the Mescaleros, who fought other Apache tribes to maintain Spanish good will, the new policy explicitly called for executing peace agreements with Apaches willing to settle at frontier military posts. Spanish troops would sweep through Apache country unceasingly on search-and-destroy missions to roust out and exterminate all who would not surrender.

Gálvez envisioned solving the Spanish Apache problem once and for all. Once the Mescaleros and other tribes settled, they were to be kept peaceful by food rations, tobacco and intoxicants. Spanish policy aimed to eliminate Apaches as enemies by extermination or debauchment.

The Spaniards initially offered Mescaleros the same rations their soldiers received — maize, wheat, beans, tobacco and semi-refined brown sugar. Like other Apaches, the Mescaleros quickly persuaded royal officials to add cattle to their rations. They were not sedentary agriculturalists, but active, meat-eating hunters and warriors. Post commanders found it expedient to issue Mescalero band chiefs licenses to take their men out hunting to supplement rations or actually to live miles from the El Paso del Norte post in sheltering mountains.

This provided further learning opportunities for the Mescalero warriors, because the Spaniards eventually issued them guns (of a quality inferior to that of Spanish garrison arms). Thus, hunter-warriors practiced marksmanship while hunting, and kept their diet adequate in terms of animal protein.⁴ Service as Indian scouts and leaders of licensed hunting expeditions strengthened the authority of Mescalero band chiefs. Marks of Spanish recognition of individual leadership reinforced the chief's authority among his fellow tribesmen much as success in economic raiding reinforced it during the previous half-century. Mescalero leaders acquired, in other words, an outside sanction for their tribal authority in the person of Spanish army officers who decided on peace or war, making diplomacy the first qualification for a Mescalero leader. Officers also approved ration issues and hunting leaves; and on rare occasions high officials even bestowed the King's silver medallion symbolizing allegiance upon outstanding Indian chiefs. The Mescaleros who forged an alliance with the Spaniards numbered eight bands under chiefs known in Spanish as Bigotes or "Mustache," Cuerno Verde or "Green Horn," Montera Blanca or "White Cap," El Quemado or "Burnt," Patule El Grande or "Big Patule," Zapato Tuerto or "Twisted Moccasin," Alegre or "Happy" and Volante or "Rover." Some died, killed by Mescalero Indian scouts as renegades, but the tribe maintained its eight-band organization through the viccissitudes of alternating service as

29

scouts for the El Paso, Monclova and San Carlos garrisons, and economic raiding at the risk of Spanish attack until Mescalero diplomacy won through a thicket of colonial official in-fighting to a lasting peace in 1790. Meanwhile, Spanish treachery in 1789 imprisoned Zapato Tuerto, Patule and El Quemado at Santa Rosa, where they died. Mescaleros had little choice, and in 1790 they achieved peace and became scouts for the Spaniards.

Mescalero women suffered a decline in prestige relative to their menfolk. They had to learn how to cook strange wheat flour, imitating the tortillas of Mexican women in the garrisons. Later, they learned to sprout maize kernels in the dark, chew them up and spit the pulp into pots to heat slowly so the mass would ferment into alcoholic *tiswin* (a general Mexican term) or *tulapai*. They learned how to sew manufactured cloth into full Spanish-style skirts and loose Spanish-style blouses and to wear them so as to avoid offending the tender moral sensibilities of Spanish Roman Catholic priests and military officers who had to answer to the priests in the confessional.

At the same time, Spanish soldiers and civilians were not loath to enjoy the semi-nudity of Mescalero women. They turned active seducers, employing – though with little success – blandishments of cash, food, cloth, and liquor tradeable for sexual favors. Thus, Mescalero

30

Photograph by Tom Mullarky, Courtesy Museum of New Mexico

A MESCALERO APACHE WOMAN, "Hattie Tom" wearing largely Spanish style clothing: a very full, long skirt; long but loose blouse, blanket caught with a clasp over the breast, necklace. Her beaded choker she may well have fashioned herself. The Apache-style basket beside her in this studio portrait may or may not have been woven by a Mescalero woman.

women faced all of Western Civilization's crass temptations in the enforced idleness and boredom of camps near the frontier forts.

Part of their answer to boredom was, not promiscuity, but to take up gambling with Spanish playing cards. The aboriginal cradleboard kept infants happy strapped to a tree branch to joggle in the breeze while mother gambled, just as it had when she worked at cutting and trimming *agave* hearts to roast.

Mescalero men also learned new social roles from the Spaniards. They saw how Spanish officers and soldiers disdained manual labor and took pride in bearing arms. So Mescalero Indian scouts gradually shared more and more their mentors' attitude of superiority relative to artisans, peasant cultivators and shepherds. At the same time, Mescalero men found congenial the fundamental Spanish individualism.

Life in close proximity to Spanish settlements exposed Mescaleros to epidemics that swept through New Spain from time to time. A growing fear of contagion probably reinforced an aboriginal tendency to bury bodies of the dead as soon as possible after death. Usually a few older relatives washed the body, combed its hair and dressed it in its finest clothing. After exposure to Christianity, at least, Mescalero mourners marked the forehead of the deceased with pollen in the form of a cross, although the face of a young person who died of a painful

32

ailment might be covered with red ochre or pollen. A burial party interred the body, wrapped in a blanket, with the head toward the west, in a grave far from camp. Mourners buried some personal property with the body, destroying the rest of the deceased person's possessions, including the horse that carried the body to its final resting place. When horses were in short supply, mourners might dock the tails of other mounts of the dead man and present them to unrelated friends.

Members of a burial party protected themselves with sage against the ghost on their departure from the grave. After Christian contact, they drew an imaginary cross on their own bodies with this "ghost medicine" plant before laying it on the grave, for the Mescalero people found ghosts frightening and dangerous at best. Ghost-fearful Mescaleros also employed ashes, spittle crosses on the forehead, black flint knives under the pillow, and pre-historic Pueblo white shell beads to fend off ghosts. They hoped the ghost would be satisfied in the afterworld paradise under ground.

An exception occurred when a Mescalero lived to a "ripe" old age. Then relatives wished for a similar longevity for themselves while handling the corpse without fear.

Masked clown dancers likely gained importance during this period of exposure to epidemic disease, because they danced when an epidemic

33

was anticipated so that one of them could obtain supernatural instructions for combatting the disease. In the shadow of Spanish forts, Mescaleros also learned some European witchcraft to add to their own aboriginal fear of malevolent witches.

PROFESSIONAL RAIDING FROM 1825 TO 1850

In time, the goals of Spanish colonial administrators might well have been achieved had Napoleon not intervened in Spain. The Mescaleros and other Apaches living on royal rations on New Spain's frontier did not disappear into the general population because New Spain became Mexico in 1821. Mexico faced grave problems in establishing mechanisms for political succession, and its resources poured into struggles for power in Mexico City. Rations and subsidies for Mescaleros and other Apaches living peacefully at frontier military posts diminished and ultimately disappeared.

Willing as they were to live on government largess, Mescaleros perforce turned to hunting, *agave* roasting and wild food gathering. Boisterous younger warriors experimented with economic raiding to express dissatisfaction with shabby treatment. Then officials placed the worst interpretation on such raids, and reverted to the pre-1786 racist Apache extermination

34

policy. Events moved in a vicious circle, and the Mescalero people finally abandoned their peaceful camps and fled northward. The year 1825 may be taken as a convenient turning point from a half century of peace to a quarter century of economic raiding of Mexican settlements.

By 1825, the westward advance of the United States gave Comanches and other Great Plains tribes other raiding targets and other military preoccupations than Mescaleros. Thus, the latter could return to an independent life in southern New Mexico and West Texas. They followed customs profoundly altered by their intimate association with Spaniards. The Mescalero people were much better equipped in 1825 to gain a livelihood from their territory than they had been in 1775. They returned to their mountains knowing how to irrigate crops on a fairly large scale. Not only could they raise maize, beans, squash and other vegetables and condiments to subsist themselves, but they also produced a maize surplus to ferment into home-brewed *tulapai* to drink to lighten the burdens of country life.

The Mescaleros herded large numbers of horses and mules, having learned the elements of animal husbandry. They carried guns and ammunition. Most importantly, they spoke barracks Spanish after a fashion and wore Mexican clothing. They had established trading relationships with villagers in many parts of northern

Mexico where they could obtain new guns and replace powder, balls and cartridges. They could, in fact, don full Mexican costume to enter carefully selected settlements to trade horses, hides and slaves for ammunition, liquor, clothing and other needed articles.

The Mescalero people painstakingly maintained good trading relationships with numerous markets so they could raid in one province and sell plunder in another. Mescaleros knew the value of the silver *peso*, and frequently dealt in cash. Because a leader bore *Peso* as a personal name, and Mescaleros so feared ghosts that they avoided uttering the name of a dead person, they substituted the equivalent but more general Spanish *dinero* ("money") after the chief's death. This also kept people from insulting relatives of a dead person who bore the name of something as common as coins. Such an insult could easily set off mortal conflict and enduring feuds.

Mescalero bands turned to economic raiding on a sophisticated, professional basis. They worked at raiding to supply their needs directly, and to convert plunder into cash. Having worked as scouts for half a century, Mescalero raiders knew every road, trail and settlement in half of northern Mexico. They were very familiar with food resources. When they spoke of Mexicans as their shepherds, Mescaleros had very specific ranches firmly in mind — they knew exactly where to go to harvest the increase in flocks Mexicans tended for them!

With half a century's experience with the Spanish army behind them, Mescalero professional raiders had long since learned European battle tactics. They also well understood the psychology of Mexican soldiers through years of close association and minute observation. All that information had been a mystery to pre-1775 Mescaleros, but their descendents turned it to very good account after 1825. Moreover, the Mescaleros became quite able at gathering up-to-date intelligence about Mexican defensive plans, troop movements, etc. Using their trading partners in Mexican provinces, the Mescaleros set up and maintained a fine "Fifth Column" long before that term was coined. Speaking Spanish to Mexican business associates, often known by Spanish names, costumed in rural Mexican style, Mescaleros could collect vital information openly and if need be infiltrate hostile settlements to analyze barroom gossip. The Gálvez policy of corrupting Apaches turned full circle when they passed for tequila-drinking, cigarette-smoking citizens on intelligence missions.

With increased technical mastery of the natural environment, and good sociological mastery of the human environment, the Mescalero people enjoyed considerable prosperity after 1825. Enjoying a free life centered on cool, well-watered mountain peaks, they grew bountiful crops, acquired livestock grown for them by Mexicans on a large scale, ate well, drank much, and dressed somewhat elegantly. Once again, male Mescaleros lightened the burdens of their matrilineal inheritance system and mother-in-law taboos. They captured and brought to camp attractive young Mexican women. After all, no mother-in-law is easier to avoid than one living hundreds of miles away, or left dead during a raid. Still, Mescalero warriors rode military escort when their women went mescal roasting, so as to protect them from Mexican, Comanche, or other hostile attack.

As professional economic raiders, Mescaleros likely held less fear of their own curers, whose witchcraft potential dimished. Raiders suffered some, though not many casualties. Moreover, years of association with Spaniards taught the Mescalero people something of the value of Western medicine. On occasion, wounded raiders obtained professional medical treatment in towns where they traded, and they employed Spanish home remedies.

Chieftainship probably declined, because any warrior could propose and organize a raid. Yet chiefs achieved considerable continuity of leadership.

The Mescalero people and other Apaches appeared well on their way to military mastery of northern Mexico when U. S. troops intervened. The United States went to war against Mexico in 1846, and U. S. forces quickly conquered the Province of New Mexico before advancing to California. Mescaleros seem to have stayed out of the way of U. S. forces during the Mexican War. When the U. S. annexed New Mexico under terms of the 1848 Treaty of Guadalupe Hidalgo, the new sovereigns had not yet identified the Mescalero people as a significant part of the military equation in the now American Southwest.

United States Amity. By 1850, at least, Mescaleros had effectively contacted U. S. forces. In September, a band from the Davis and Guadalupe Mountains rode into San Elizario, Texas, to determine American sentiments. The new officials gave them food. Mescalero chiefs Simón Manuel and Simón Porode repeated the test at El Paso, with similar results. Then, New Mexican Governor J. C. Calhoun, who also acted as Indian Agent for the Territory, signed on April 2, 1851, a treaty with a Jicarilla Apache leader and the Mescalero chiefs Josecito and Lobo (Wolf).

The next year, Indian Agent John Greiner

39

received a party of 30 Mescaleros at Santa Fé, gave them presents and a dance, and on July 1 signed another treaty with them and leaders of other Apache tribes. Although hostilities between U. S. citizens and Mescaleros began soon after, Chief Josecito and seven companions visited Santa Fé peacefully on May 31, 1853, stressing the tribe's agricultural industry and seeking a fort for mutual protection of Indians and settlers. Very possibly the excellent intelligence operations of the Mescaleros convinced them that immigrants from the eastern states were too numerous and well-armed for them to defeat. Clearly, responsible chiefs sought to establish a Mescalero-U. S. alliance from the beginning of U. S. sovereignty in New Mexico Territory.

U.S. Hostility. The Mescalero quest for allegiance with the United States failed. A new territorial governor sworn in at the national capital on May 22, 1853, reached Santa Fé in August. Kentuckian David Meriwether followed federal policy of rationing New Mexico's native Americans and bestowing presidential allegiance medals and great coats on tribal chiefs who cooperated, or militarily attacking them if they did not. Justification for military action against Mescaleros came easily. Some bands living in northern Mexico raided immigrants on the San Antonio-El Paso road. More than a quarter century of profitable professional raiding had set

40

a lasting pattern of raiding band leadership. Professional raiders followed raiding band chiefs whose planning and execution of raids was most effective. Tribal leadership suffered as raiding band leadership strengthened, so no Mescalero could speak for all his people, much less exercise central authority over them. The tendency of U. S. citizens to lump all Indians together, and their initial ignorance of details of tribal or band organization, meant that all Mescaleros suffered reprisals for what whites considered depredations by any Mescalero — indeed, by almost any Apache.

Through 1854, U. S. troop strength built up in the territory. U. S. officials estimated 750 Mescaleros occupied land east of the Río Grande past the Río Pecos north to the 34th parallel. At the end of the year, Capt. R. S. Ewell led 80 men out of Ft. Thorn to invade the Mescalero core territory. In mid-January, Ewell's command climbed the eastern slope of the Sacramento Mountains, where Mescalero warriors commenced to delay them with nighttime arrow attacks supplemented with such firearms as they possessed, and setting fire to dry grass. On January 18, 1855, Ewell reached the settlements warriors tried to defend. He ordered Capt. H. W. Stanton to reconnoiter a second tipi group. Well-mounted, Stanton out-charged his men in pursuit of some fleeing Mescaleros. Returning to the main force, Stanton fell in an ambush. Thus,

41

Mescalero warriors provided the U. S. with another name for a frontier military post.

Ewell pursued the Mescaleros to the summit of the 9,000 foot high range before turning north toward the Manzano Mountains under intermittent attack. His search-and-destroy mission succeeded in driving the entire tribe out of its winter settlement without food or shelter, and inflicting numerous casualties during many skirmishes. Their pride crushed, one group of 15 warriors followed Ewell back to Ft. Thorn. On February 23, they attacked the four men guarding the horse-herd 25 miles from the post, wounding every guard at least four times. Nine other Mescaleros stole all the livestock from a settlement 20 miles south of Santa Fé that same month. With eight soldiers and eight citizens, Lt. S. D. Sturgis pursued and killed nine raiders by a charge and recovered the stock.

U. S. Amity. The U. S. cavalry succeeded, as royal Spanish dragoons had decades earlier, in persuading Mescaleros to sue for peace. Dr. Michael Steck had become their Agent. He was able to restrain cavalry officers from further missions in Mescalero country, and with Governor Meriwether to negotiate a treaty with the Mescalero chiefs. They agreed to restrict their people to an Indian reservation similar in size and location to the present Mescalero Indian Reservation. Congress never ratified the June 14, 1855, treaty, however, so Mescaleros lived for

42

years under the illusion that they enjoyed a treaty allegiance to the U. S. that did not in fact exist.

The War Department established a military post at the junction of Ruidoso and Bonito Rivers in May, 1855. Built to overawe the Mescalero people, this Ft. Stanton was named for the officer killed in battle by those native Americans.

So effective had the cavalry's search-and-destroy missions been that even Gov. Meriwether was moved to pity when he saw the condition of Mescaleros at Ft. Thorn during treaty negotiations. He himself had rations issued, and ordered Agent Steck to continue such issues in the future when Mescaleros requested relief and appeared to need it.

Faced with continued economic raiding — and certainly Mescalero professional raiders were destitute enough to brave the entire U. S. Army — Steck demanded that stolen property be returned before he issued more rations. Mescaleros held out in the Sierra Blanca as long as they could, scavenging dead mules at Ft. Thorn. In November, 1856, Steck met Mescaleros at Ft. Stanton to hand out blankets, shirts, knives, tobacco and provisions. He promised five beeves and 30 Spanish bushels of maize once a lunar month. Meanwhile, Steck had taken a step toward what would today be called "community development" among the destitute exprofessional raiders. In the spring of 1856, he hired six men to start a farming project in La Luz Canyon at the foot of the Sacramento Mountains. They planted 70 acres to maize and vegetables.

Chief Cadete assured U. S. officials that he would prevent further "depredations," helping his Mescalero followers to make a virtue of necessity. Cadete's father, Chief Barranquito, probably represented the generation of professional raiding band leaders who found it extremely difficult if not impossible to accept the fact that the Mescalero people had been so decisively defeated that the prosperous life-way followed between 1825 and 1850 was no longer possible. The peaceful path proved strewn with stones. New Mexican citizens attacked peaceful Mescaleros twice, but other bands stood off cavalry detachments at Carrizozo and Dog Canyon in the Sacramento Mountains.

Poverty and hunger once again sent Mescalero women out to sunny slopes where *agave* grew abundantly to cut edible plants off their roots, trim off spines, and fire up the pits to roast them so their families might survive. Farms at Alamargordo or on the Peñasco River and government rations failed to feed the people adequately up to 1860.

Confederate Enmity. While the Mescalero people struggled to learn another European language, English, and used every bit of their

44

FORT STANTON, New Mexico Territory, in 1885. Two companies of the 13th U.S. Infantry on parade. U.S. frontier posts typically consisted of comfortable buildings erected around a parade ground without external fortifications, as shown in this view.

hand-won knowledge of Southwestern game animals and food-producing plants to survive, far-away events plunged them into the maelstrom of armed conflict with better-armed and more numerous whites. Sectional rivalries and controversies plunged the Anglo-Americans who had recently ousted Mexican officials from New Mexico into civil war among themselves. A Confederate army organized in Texas marched on New Mexico Territory, occupying Ft. Bliss at El Paso and Ft. Fillmore near Las Cruces, N.M. The Texans marched north up the Río Grande to defeat Union forces in battle at Val Verde before loyal troops halted their advance in Glorieta Pass.

The federal commander at Ft. Stanton retreated to Albuquerque as soon as he learned that Ft. Fillmore's commander had surrendered to the Confederates. He fired the post, but rain put out the fire. Local New Mexican settlers and Mescaleros quickly salvaged undamaged stores. Possibly understanding the racial views of the Confederacy, possibly simply scornful of inept military field performance, Mescaleros killed three men of a four-man patrol scouting north from the Sierra Blanca range. They then attacked settlers at Placitas (modern Lincoln), but were repulsed by the Confederates. When the Texan lieutenant in command pulled back to Doña Ana, however, the settlers quickly abandoned their homes near Ft. Stanton.

Once again the Mescalero people occupied their country. Raiders took up their old stands to ambush wagon trains along the southern immigrant road through El Paso. They began killing settlers, driving off horses, mules, donkeys, cattle and sheep, and taking captives.

U. S. Conquest. The renewed independence of the Mescalero people vanished before it was well established. A powerful California Volunteer force reached the Rio Grande in July, 1862, just a bit tardy to engage retreating Confederate forces. General James H. Carleton commanded this California Column. Whatever Mescalero band chiefs may have thought about enmity between Confederate and Union forces, Carleton soon demonstrated that racial unity among Anglo-Americans outweighed their divisions. Carleton defined pacification of Indians in New Mexico Territory as his top priority after the departure of the Confederates. On September 27, 1862, Carleton ordered Volunteer Colonel Christopher Carson to reoccupy Ft. Stanton with five companies of his regiment. Moreover, the general ordered Carson to kill Mescalero men "wherever you can find them," but to capture and feed their women and children until their chiefs and 20 principal men went to Santa Fé to sue for peace. Subordinate officers carried out Carleton's orders to attack the Mescalero people from north, west and southwest. In October, Capt. James Graydon had his command open fire on Chief Manuelito, who had his hand raised as a sign of truce, slaying five other men and one woman. His troops killed five more men and wounded others when the Mescaleros fled.

As such officers led volunteer forces through Mescalero country, survivors fled to Ft. Stanton and the protection of Col. Carson. That able frontiersman in late November dispatched five Mescalero spokesmen under military escort to the territorial capital. Indian Agent Lorenzo Labadi accompanied them. Cadete asked the Governor for peace, admitting defeat, but requesting consideration for Mescalero warriors as "men and braves."

Gen. Carleton turned out to be a staunch practitioner of Indian removal. On November 4, he had already issued orders to establish a new post near Bosque Redondo on the Pecos River. Called Ft. Sumner, this post was to be a concentration camp for surrendered native Americans in the territory. The defeated Mescalero bands became its first prisoners. Carleton promised Cadete and his companions that their people would be fed at Ft. Sumner as long as their behavior suited Carleton's exacting expectations. With little choice, the Mescalero people made their tearful trek into internment. Over 400 Mescaleros drew rations — beef, maize, wheat, kraut, pickles or rice, peas, dried fruit and salt — at Ft. Sumner by mid-March, 1863.

Perhaps 100 others fled west to fight beside the Gila Apaches, or became refugees in Mexico.

Those at Ft. Sumner settled down to lay out fields and plant crops, mostly maize, pumpkins and melons, and build ramshackle housing. After Indians massacred a party of Mexican salt gatherers west of Ft. Stanton, Carleton ordered commanders of both that post and Ft. Sumner to shoot on sight any Mescalero not interned. If those interned caused trouble, Carleton ordered them disarmed and their horses confiscated.

Gen. J. H. Carleton directed the manpower under his righteous command not only against Mescaleros but also against other native Americans in New Mexico Territory. Carson's territorial volunteers began making headway in resource attrition in Navajo country following the Mescalero defeat and internment. In September, 1863, Carleton's officers dispatched a first contingent of defeated Navajos to internment at Ft. Sumner.

By the time U. S. troops finished their search-and-destroy missions in Navajo territory, almost 9,000 Navajos had made their Long Walk to Ft. Sumner. Thinking that they would be the only prisoners at the post, the Mescalero people resented the Navajos.

Agent Lorenzo Labadi struggled to achieve some improvement in treatment of 472 Mescalero interned people whom neither War Department nor Interior Department officials wanted to feed. He complained in 1865 that interned Indians were fed beef from cattle dying of disease. Gen. Carleton, who previously praised Labadi, ordered him expelled from the internment camp on the pretext that the agent had purchased cattle to feed the Indians.

Capt. John C. Cremony of the California Volunteers sought to license Mescalero hunters to supplement their food supplies. Carleton disapproved, even after Mescaleros bagged 87 antelope during one 48-hour hunt Cremony managed to set up. Carleton would not even allow women to roast *agave* hearts, the immemorial mainstay when food ran short.

Virtually the only safety valve available to frustrated and often physically ill Mescalero warriors was an occasional battle with Navajos. Many of the latter escaped internment and raided New Mexican settlements. In December of 1863, Agent Labadi led 30 Mescaleros under Chiefs Cadete and Ojo Blanco ("White Eye") 26 miles along the trail of a renegade Navajo band with stolen sheep and defeated the raiders during a four hour battle. Twelve Navajos died to one Mescalero and the combined force recovered 9,889 sheep.

On January 4, 1864, Navajos stole 60 Mescalero horses and army mounts as well. Labadi mustered 60 Mescaleros under Chief Ojo Blanco and the army sent 15 men. After nine hours on the trail, the pursuers overtook the

Navajos, who selected the battleground. Nonetheless, the Mescalero-Army force killed 52 of 120 Navajos engaged. The rest escaped after dark. By the fall of 1864, even Apachephobe Carleton approved recruiting 30 Mescaleros under Chief Cadete as scouts against the Kiowa Indians.

Deadly enmity between Navajos and Mescaleros kept the latter nervous. Toward the end of May, 1864, Chief Ojo Blanco fled with 42 people to Mescalero country. Lorenzo Labadi warned him by messenger that he could not be protected there, and Ojo Blanco returned to internment in August with 60 followers.

During the summers of 1864 and 1865, weather conditions and crop pests ended any prospect of a successful harvest of maize planted at Ft. Sumner. In the summer of 1864, the 94 Mescalero gardeners did sell $4,000 worth of melons, green beans, peppers and other truck. The approaching climax of the war in the East actually diminished supplies available in the West. Carleton cut the bread ration to three-quarters of a pound daily and the meat to half a pound per person in 1864 and to half a pound of bread with a pound and a quarter of meat in 1865. As they had when Mexico diminished their rations, Mescaleros chose to return to freedom to survive. On the night of November 3, 1865, every Mescalero save for sick or crippled individuals vanished from the internment camp.

Recognizing the realities of the situation, the people scattered. They probably broke their subsistence parties down into minimum extended family camps. Some headed into the Sierra Blanca; others braved the southern Great Plains to forge a temporary alliance with the ancient Comanche enemy. Most Mescaleros simply disappeared from Anglo-American sight for seven years. During this refugee period, Mescaleros in contact with Lipan Apaches learned from them to conduct curing ceremonies centered upon peyote, a cactus that acts as a hallucigen when ingested. The two tribes combined against their common enemies.

No later than 1867, Chief Santana returned to the Sierra Blanca. His band eked out a living by its own horticultural and hunting efforts, and he endeavored to keep hostile bands away from the area of the unratified treaty reservation.

By 1869, Lt. A. G. Hennissee was detailed to care for the Sierra Blanca Mescaleros. He recommended that the U. S. legally re-establish the reservation specified in the unratified treaty, and began negotiating with band chiefs about peaceful settlement. Ft. Stanton troops captured a couple of Mescalero women the post commandant treated well and sent out to persuade their tribesmen to settle at the fort. In February, 1870, José La Paz ("Joseph the Peace") brought a small band in. These Mescaleros worked to some extent with military details cultivating crops, including maize for sale to the army. Santana apparently backed the minor chief from the background, testing Anglo-American sincerity. Sent to the Great Plains to contact refugee Mescaleros, José La Paz returned in April with 30 of them, and with Chief Cadete's message that his people would return to the homeland when there was grass enough on the Staked Plains for them to cross.

That summer Cadete did bring his people across the Pecos River into Ft. Stanton. There a new agent, Unitarian A. J. Curtis, in 1871 joined in a council to agree on U. S. government protection for the Mescaleros, a school for their children, and fields to cultivate. The Mescalero people were to retain their livestock and all property then in their possession. The great leader who long acted as principal spokesman for the Mescalero people in dealings with Anglo-Americans was murdered two years later returning from Mesilla. By that time, 830 Mescalero Apaches lived near Ft. Stanton.

A CENTURY OF RESERVATION DEVELOPMENT

Lt. Hennissee's recommendation that the un-ratified treaty reservation be legalized fit into the temper of native American administration under President U. S. Grant. As part of a massive post-war effort at pacification of hostile tribes and creation of orderly United States administration of those pacified, Grant dispatched a personal emisary, Vincent Colyer, to study the situation in the Southwest. Although Colyer did not visit the then-peaceful Mescalero people, he did recommend that the U. S. establish for them a reservation in their ancestral territory near Ft. Stanton.

On May 29, 1873, President U. S. Grant signed an Executive Order creating the Mescalero Indian Reservation. He reserved for these people a tract bounded by a line running south from Ft. Stanton to the 33d parallel (except for an area around white settlements) to the top of the Sacramento Mountains, to the top of the Sierra Blanca to the headwaters of the Rio Nogal and the fort. Thus, the United States finally brought the Mescalero people within the somewhat stabilizing influence of its one stable policy, that of segregating native Americans from citizens.

Turmoil and Uncertainty, 1873-1881. The President of the United States might decree that land be reserved to the Mescalero people, but Washington's writ did not always run in New Mexico Territory. The Mescalero people remained suspended in a social and economic condition of great uncertainty and psychological stress for a number of years after Grant set aside their reservation.

For one thing, the boundaries of the reserved

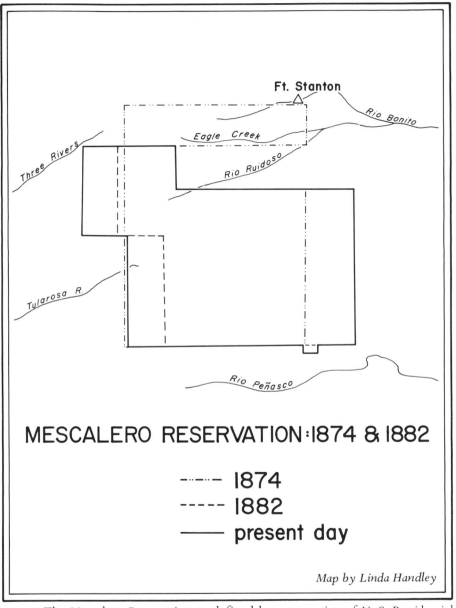

Ft. Stanton

Rio Bonito

Three Rivers

Eagle Creek

Rio Ruidoso

Tularosa R.

Rio Peñasco

MESCALERO RESERVATION:1874 & 1882

–··– 1874
----- 1882
—— present day

Map by Linda Handley

MAP 3. The Mescalero Reservation as defined by a succession of U. S. Presidential Executive Orders in 1874, 1882 and 1883.

area remained long unsurveyed and uncertain. Consequently, neither the Mescalero people nor anyone else knew just where they lay. Because hostilities continued between U. S. troops and other hostile native Americans, Mescaleros dared not venture beyond undefined boundaries to hunt or roast mescal for fear they would be shot as renegades. Thus, they rotted in idleness, dependent on government rations once they virtually exterminated game within the area considered safe for hunting.

To complicate matters even more, a number of hard-case whites had taken up claims to arable lands within the reserved area during Mescalero internment at Ft. Sumner. Once the Mescalero people settled on the reserved area, many of these squatters peddled them what passed for whiskey or operated gambling games to relieve them of any monetary resources not spent on rot-gut liquor. Indian agents honestly trying to perform their duties had no jurisdiction over such islands of Anglo-American private property within the reservation.

Not all agents were even trying honestly to perform their duties. Some were dishonestly committed to lining their own pockets with cash at Mescalero expense.

Once Mescaleros attempted to settle on their reservation, they became the targets of depredations by covetous Anglo-Americans and massacres by Indian-hating soldiers. For six years after the Executive Order established the Mescalero Reservation, its inhabitants lived in constant danger from troops and desperadoes.

In September of 1873, for example, Major W. R. Price, acting on white settlers' complaints, arrested Chiefs Santana and Román. He told them that they would be held hostage until stolen horses were returned. So 200 Mescaleros fled, some to the Comanches, some to Mexico. One of Price's officers attacked a Mescalero camp, killing seven men, women, and children.

On February 2, 1874, President Grant redefined the reservation boundary as running due west from Ft. Stanton to the Sierra Blanca summit, then south to the 33d parallel, east to a point south of the fort and then north to it with a big jog to leave out existing white settlements, a 570,240 acre reserved area.

The next fall, a gang of whites fired on a Mescalero camp, killing several women and children, and drove off the Indians' horses. They repeated this feat the next January. The best the commandant of Ft. Stanton would do was to encourage the Mescalero people to live within gunshot of his post.

When thoroughly frightened Mescaleros scattered, troops pursued them. Capt. E. G. Fechet's command surprised a band camped in a canyon and opened fire. The Mescaleros abandoned all their possessions in flight. An agency employee and two citizens found some starving survivors two weeks later and persuaded them to return and grow maize, beans and squash. Others kept going to Mexico.

President Grant on October 20, 1875, again tried to define the boundary of the reservation. Nonetheless, the Mescalero people, nearly all of whom still spoke Spanish as well as Southern Athapascan, settled down again. Chiefs requested schools for their children. They farmed irrigated fields despite damage from stock of passing travelers. At times trading a horse or mule for a quart of whiskey, they drank heavily with serious consequences. For example, those Warm Springs Apaches intermarried with Mescaleros fled the reservation after a drunken brawl.

On top of all else, epidemic smallpox struck the Mescalero people in the winter of 1876. Chief Santana, who had led his people since 1830 and exercised a moderating influence after Barranquito's death in 1857, caught the disease. Dr. J. H. Blazer, who had purchased a sawmill within the reservation, brought the chief into his house to nurse him through his illness. Santana returned to his home during Blazer's temporary absence, contracted pneumonia, and died. Some considered him "the last real chief of the Mescaleros," but Nautzili and Pinole effectively led the two largest bands the next year. Epidemic mortality among the Mescalero people ran high, and the population plummeted. Yet the government opened a school on South Fork in January, 1877, rather than a hospital.

Gyrations of U. S. Apache policy continued, to the further cost of the Mescalero people. In May, 1877, the government moved 453 unhappy Warm Springs Apaches from their 1874 reservation, which President R. B. Hayes returned to the public domain, to San Carlos as part of an Apache concentration policy. That fall 260 received permission to return to Warm Springs. In August, 1878, troops arrived to take them back to San Carlos, but Victorio decamped at the head of 80 men. While he headed for Mexico, old Chief Nana led 63 men to the Mescalero reservation in December. For their own safety from white desperadoes, Mescalero band chiefs Estrella ("Star") and Peso visited the agency only when hungry enough to take the risk.

The following June 30th, Victorio brought his 13 men there also. Dr. Blazer killed one of his own steers to feed them and provided the refugees with sugar, coffee and flour to keep the Warm Springs warriors at peace. During a government ration issue, the agent nervously sent to Ft. Stanton for troop protection. A bugler played a call as the detachment approached Blazer's Mill, and set off six years of epic guerrilla warfare. Within minutes, Victorio and his followers mounted. The leader shook hands with Dr. Blazer in sad farewell and took the war trail, slaying two sheep herders for their horses before he even left the reservation. Some discontented Mescalero professional raiders joined him. By the spring of 1880, an Indian agent estimated that 250 Mescaleros rode with Victorio's fantastically successful guerrilla force.

Mescalero participation in Victorio's bloodying of the Anglo-American frontier brought down upon the peaceful Mescaleros who remained on their reservation the frustrated wrath of the U. S. Army. Colonel Edward Hatch notified Agent S. A. Russell that he would consider as hostile all Indians not at the agency on April 12th with all their stock. Russell brought all the Mescaleros within a hour's ride of the agency by April 10th. When the Mescaleros saw 1,000 troops ride up, all but one encampment disappeared. The senior officer informed the agent that he meant to disarm and unhorse the Mescalero people. The agent enlisted Chiefs Nautzile, San Juan, Griego ("The Greek") and Román to bring in the 400 people remaining on the reservation by April 16th, and labored hard to prevent an army massacre of Mescalero hunters out on an authorized hunt.

On the fatal day, Agent Russell bravely undertook personally to collect the men's arms. A few Apaches handed over their arms. Others drifted away, and the troops opened fire on them, killing 14. Survivors were searched, their horses confiscated, and they were incarcerated

Photograph by Ben Wittick, Courtesy Museum of New Mexico

MESCALERO APACHE CHIEFS SAN JUAN AND NAUTZILI (seated) photographed in a Santa Fé studio, probably in 1882. Chief San Juan wears a large U.S. presidential Peace Medal pinned under a smaller medal on his vest, showing the bust of the president. He wears metal earrings, and both chiefs wear finger-rings on their left hands. Nautzili sports a single claw on his necklace.

in an old horse corral covered with several inches of manure, a crowning indignity.

Cavalry patrols killed several small groups of Mescaleros who had escaped the first disarmament massacre. Col. Edward Hatch encamped his troops at the agency, so the Mescalero people there dared not move. In September, Hatch allowed them to range eight miles from the agency, but not to approach white-owned ranches or use the roads. Not until January, 1881, did troops withdraw from the reservation, having created enduring bitterness among surviving Mescaleros.

Prologue to Progress, 1881-1883. On June 16, 1881, W. H. H. Llewellyn arrived as U. S. Indian Agent to the Mescalero people. A remarkable individual, Llewellyn took the first positive steps toward building a new Mescalero social structure on the reservation the Commissioner of Indian Affairs wanted to abandon. Seeking behavior that would enable Mescaleros to survive under the drastically altered conditions of U. S. dominance, Llewellyn quickly attacked age-old Mescalero cultural customs that he found incompatible with Anglo-American values. Yet Llewellyn maintained his perspective, refusing to condemn automatically such customs as mother-in-law avoidance. When parents of newborn twins brought them to the agent to decide which one to kill, he interdicted the ancient custom.

Just as quickly as he could, Llewellyn followed San Carlos Agent John Clum's lead and established a Mescalero police force for the reservation. He initially enlisted 15 Mescaleros under command of Captain Thomas Branigan of Las Cruces, an action that stabilized reservation conditions more than any previous Bureau of Indian Affairs move. Sam Chino, one of the original policemen, typified the new leadership that exhorted the people to take "the right direction."

Llewellyn also assigned three Mescaleros to herd agency stock and hired others to subjugate 50 acres of farmland. Over a two-year period, he claimed that he taught 20 men to plow, but when Llewellyn arrived 147 families already grew "Mexican" type quick-maturing maize adapted to the 6,000-foot elevation. They also traded beautiful willow baskets women made to Mexican orchardists for peaches, grapes, etc.

In 1882, Llewellyn could report that he had added a doctor to the agency staff, hired five more Indian policemen, brought 70 acres into cultivation, held a day school in session for a full term for the first time, sent Mescalero children to Albuquerque to school for the first time, and erected two log houses. Llewellyn became the first of many agents who over-invested in Anglo-American style housing for people who so feared the ghosts of the dead that they moved camp and abandoned and burned a dwelling when someone died, just as they discarded household

63

goods frequently handled by the deceased. To continue to use them would invite the ghost to visit survivors.

The physician was able to vaccinate 580 Mescaleros against smallpox in the winter of 1881-82, and nearly all the rest the next winter, thus reducing epidemic deaths. This effect was masked by other illnesses, military defeat and enforced idleness which magnified Mescalero fears of death, so accusations of witchcraft increased. In 1881, reservation residents burned a woman as a witch, although the agent did not find this out for many months. When he did, he prohibited such executions. Llewellyn knew enough history to point out that the Mescalero people lagged only somewhat more than a century behind the Puritans in this regard.

The Mescalero people witnessed in 1882 another shift in federal policy toward them. White prospectors located some likely colors in a portion of the reservation, and clamored for it to be placed in the public domain. The Chester A. Arthur administration acceded on May 19th, giving the miners a six-by-15 mile strip on the southwest and adding a strip nine by 21 miles on the east to provide more grazing land for the Mescalero people. They ended up with a 472,320 acre reserve. The President re-defined the boundary on 24 March, 1883.

Despite these federal concessions to non-Indians, 50 Mescaleros visited Santa Fé for its

Photograph by Ben Wittick, Courtesy Museum of New Mexico

MESCALERO APACHES CHIEFS SAN JUAN AND NAUTZILI seated in the Mescalero encampment at the Santa Fé, New Mexico, "tertio-millennial" celebration in the early 1880's. Chief San Juan wears what appears to be a U.S. presidential Peace Medal pinned to his vest. He holds a bow in its case, and a handfull of arrows. Chief Nautzili holds a Mescalero cavalry lance. The weapons tripods behind the two chiefs hold circular Mescalero war shields with painted designs, cased bows and lances.

"tertio-millennial" celebration. When, moreover, a Roman Catholic missionary visited the reservation in 1883, Mescalero memory of Spanish Catholicism remained so strong that he could baptize no less than 173 individuals. Even more unbelievably, ten Mescaleros had enlisted to serve with U. S. forces.

Regression, 1883-1887. Another vagary of federal Apache policy in 1882 brought an order to move the Jicarilla Apaches to the Mescalero Reservation, a special inspector having decided not to move the Mescaleros elsewhere. Llewellyn supervised the transfer of 721 Jicarillas. They started their 47 day, 502 mile trip on August 20th. Six people died of smallpox on the trail, and one Jicarilla chief made no bones about his dislike for the Mescalero reserve.

On the other hand, peaceful conditions appeared to be on the horizon when Mexican troops stumbled on Victorio in 1883 and massacred his 86 warriors and 18 women and children when the Apaches' ammunition ran out.

Llewellyn purchased 500 head of cattle for the two tribes, only to find that most of them gambled cattle away and the new owners promptly butchered for beef to eat. With the enforced idleness of reservation life and the end of professional raiding, plus long-customary disdain for manual labor such as cattle herding or horticulture, Mescalero braves turned to gambling with a passion. By 1883, formal education had taught only five to read, so recreational reading offered no alternative to the vast non-literate majority. In 1884, the Bureau of Indian Affairs founded a boarding school at Mescalero Agency to replace the day school and increase school impact on pupils.

Agent F. J. Cowart, a pronounced pessimist, replaced ever-optimistic Llewellyn on November 18, 1885. By that time, the always-religious Mescaleros displayed all of the symptoms of a defeated people subject to apparently capricious actions by their conquerors, in many accusations of witchcraft. Another epidemic did not help the situation, especially when head Chief Román disregarded the doctor's advice to stay away from white communities where the contagion raged, contracted the malady and died. The new agent threatened to use the 32 Indian policemen to place in irons anyone who made accusations of witchcraft after curers who labored to save Chief San Juan accused two Lipan Apaches of having bewitched their patient.

Cowart took another step toward creating a reservation socio-political structure in the winter of 1886 by organizing a Court of Indian Offenses with both Mescalero and Jicarilla justices. Half the Mescalero men were winning Anglo-American respect by serving as U. S. Army Indian Scouts in the Geronimo campaign, rehabilitating their tribe in public opinion.

Mescalero Isolation, 1887-1895. In the fall of

67

1886, 200 Jicarilla Apaches decamped from the reservation and encamped near San Ildefonso Pueblo, refusing to return to Mescalero country. Consequently the federal government reserved for them their own reservation in May, 1887, and transferred there those Jicarillas who had remained with the Mescalero people. This left 438 Mescaleros as sole occupants of their reservation, with the opportunity to develop its resources for their own benefit. They decided to divide their tribally held herd into family property, probably in recognition of the nature of Anglo-American property concepts and law.

The local Indian Agent tried to re-fill the school after Jicarilla students departed by using Indian policemen as truant officers. He had to discharge three of them for non-cooperation and thoroughly antagonized many parents. Abortion and infanticide continued to contribute to population decline.

By 1889, some Mescalero families had entered the freighting business. Some had begun to milk their cows and to move away from agency headquarters. Three-fourths of the children attended school, and a Methodist preacher held regular monthly services at the boarding school. That spring federal authorities allowed five Mescalero families interned with Gerónimo's renegades in Florida to return to the reservation.

J. F. Bennett became Indian Agent in that year, and warned white cattlemen to stop grazing what he estimated as 8,000 head of livestock on reservation lands. Bennett measured Mescalero cultural change toward Anglo-American patterns in terms of 14 families in houses and six with stoves in their kitchens.

When Col. Hinman Rhodes succeeded Bennett as Agent in 1890, he found that after Bennett suspended the school superintendent following fisticuffs between the pair, he allowed instruction to disintegrate. Rhodes found not a single child attending class, and hired a new superintendent. By 1892, that official claimed that 35 Mescaleros could read and write, despite too many "school" hours spent maintaining school buildings, sewing clothes, and working the school farm.

Richard Hudson became agent in 1892, and Capt. Levi Burnett assumed command of the agency in 1893. He found that half the 250 cattle Llewellyn had issued survived. The parade of agents to the Mescaleros brought changing faces, unstable local policy, and a slow pace of Mescalero cultural change until Burnett's departure late in 1895.

Accelerating Forced Change, 1895-1899. On December 11, 1895, Lt. V. E. Stottler became agent to the Mescalero people, promptly accelerating the pace of forced cultural change.

From Stottler's Anglo-American point of view, Mescalero mother-in-law avoidance was a ridiculous custom, and social power of elderly female extended family heads a brake on Mescalero "progress." Whatever Stottler's ethnocentrism, he accurately identified key points in Mescalero social structure where governmental force could rapidly alter reservation life.

Many children played truant from school, hiding in the brush, chewing peyote, simulating infirmities. Stottler had the Indian police imprison their grandmothers — matriarchs in their extended families and major authority figures both generally and specifically in educating their grandchildren. He cut off their parents' rations. Stottler railed against taxing U. S. citizens to finance Mescalero ignorance, cruelty, superstition, cunning, filth, sloth, stubbornness, immorality, intemperance, mendaciousness and begging, and consciously fashioned a policy of applying "pressure" to critical points of Indian social structure to alter the situation.

Lt. Stottler not only attacked Mescalero family structure, but also attempted to destroy the four bands. He took their chiefs, who had served as judges, farmer and police chief, off the payroll and stopped giving them presents. Further, Stottler would not allow them to act as spokesmen for their people, forcing individuality on the men.

This army ogre solved a problem that plagued Indian Agents all over the country by persuading native Americans to trim their long locks, using threats judiciously. Stottler probably neither knew nor cared that short hair was a Mescalero mourning symbol. First, he increased the rations issued to Indian policemen. Then he discharged two former school students for wearing long hair, and bribed one man to cut his for $5. He pressured others with rations, and then ordered all policemen to trim their hair or be discharged. Once the Indian police force had been shorn, it eagerly compelled the general Mescalero population to cut its hair. The change took weeks only.

In accord with his Protestant ethic, Stottler enforced the concept earlier agents had enunciated of withholding rations from Mescaleros who did not work. His great project was a two-mile-long, four-foot-wide irrigation ditch for the school farm, for which he turned out every adult Indian on the reserved area for six days of forced labor. Then Stottler ordered every Mescalero man to chose some land to fence. He withheld rations until the fence was completed.

Sharing the general Christian disdain for native American ceremonies, Stottler viewed Mescalero dances as advertising mature girls for the highest bid. He prohibited native ceremonies. He also suppressed brewing *tulapai*. Earlier agents had the Indian police break up *tulapai* camps. Stottler not only broke them up, but burned them and imprisoned those Mescaleros found brewing *tulapai* for several months at hard labor. He had already abolished the native court.

In order to further the diffusion of Anglo-American culture even more, Stottler ordered all the Mescalero men to move into houses. Each man had to fell logs and somehow move them to the sawmill. Stottler in 1897 provided the first 45 finished houses with stoves and Anglo-American cooking utensils. In another assault on the traditional role of Mescalero women, Stottler in 1895 imported Navajo weavers to teach them how to make blankets, so basket-making declined. On the other hand, Stottler also encouraged female family heads in women's traditional gardening activity.

The few things Mescaleros did to Stottler's satisfaction included hauling 100 tons of agency freight annually 110 miles from the railway, performing all the labor in the sawmill under a white supervisor, and earning over $2,000 in wages per year.

By mid-1898, Mescaleros occupied 86 reservation houses compared to 14 less than a decade earlier. Stottler could measure Mescalero cultural change in things and take pride in his accomplishment.

Money and Missionaries, 1899-1918. Stottler further diversified the reservation grazing economy in 1897 by purchasing 5,000 sheep, or

A MESCALERO APACHE CAMP in Otero County, New Mexico, during the period of continued residence in canvas-covered tipis when the Mescalero people had adopted wheeled wagons for hauling burdens such as water barrels.

ten head for every person on it — under orders from the Commissioner. He also promoted the cultivation of new crops: potatoes, oats, cabbages and other vegetables besides traditional maize and pumpkins. All of Stottler's "pressures" moved the Mescalero people rapidly toward a fully cash economy, consuming foodstuffs grown or purchased from local traders. To gain a sounder economic position, some Mescaleros traded surplus ponies for sheep and goats to augment those issued by the agent. In 1899, moreover, Mescaleros sold enough agricultural produce to purchase 300 goats to add to their growing flocks. Agent W. M. Luttrell forced the people almost completely into the market economy by ending ration issues to anyone other than Indian policemen and 50 aged individuals.

In quite another sphere, Mescaleros began playing baseball by 1899, and winning, symbolizing cultural change in the direction of Anglo-American organized team sports.

In 1901, J. A. Carroll became Superintendent of the Mescalero Indian Agency to remain for a full decade, the longest tenure of any agent until that time. Possessing tremendous power over his charges, Carroll urged the Mescalero people onward at the slow process of building economic security and new social structures under severe bureaucratic restraints. They lived in real poverty on produce from their gardens, some

74

craft sales for cash and undoubtedly some meat from their flocks, which they were still building up in numbers.

By 1902, the Bureau of Indian Affairs considered Mescaleros able to support themselves. It ended its ration issues, and Carroll brought in the first bonded, licensed trader. The government improved local cash income when it began to pay men $1.25 per day or a man with a team $2.50. It also instituted the practice of making per capita payments to Mescalero individuals from tribal income from grazing fees charged white ranchers. By 1904, such permits brought in some $3,000 annually, perhaps half of which went into per capita payments. Mescalero cash income from other sources mounted. Wool and slaughter sheep sales brought in almost $12,000 in 1905-06. Under Carroll, oats became the largest reservation farm crop, yielding 400,000 pounds a year by 1906. Sales of crafts brought in $1,500 annually, against $800 from horse sales or $2,500 for farm produce. Income reached $68.85 per capita.

Mescalero population continued to decline during the early years of the century. In 1905, 37 Lipans from Mexico reinforced the Mescaleros, with whom they had already intermarried.

Probably as important as actual reinforcements in halting the numerical decline of the Mescalero people was the beginning of Christian missionary work. During a half century at Spanish forts, a few Mescaleros had actually been educated in convents, and many more learned an elemental Roman Catholicism. Yet latter-day Christian missionaries ignored the Mescalero people until 1907. The defeated tribe, forced to doubt its own traditional beliefs by crushing military defeat and consequent social subordination, poverty, and forced cultural change, received no message of hope in terms of an alternative religion during the entire first third of a century of reservation life! Missionaries of the Reformed Church began prosyletizing among the Mescaleros in 1907. In 1911, Roman Catholic missionaries finally returned to convert the people Spanish-speaking priests had instructed between 1775 and 1825. The Christian message the missionaries brought at least offered some Mescaleros an opportunity to improve their morale by believing in salvation and behaving in terms of a Christian ethic.

Just as Christian optimism first became available to the Mescalero people, their reservation land base again came under attack. On March 2, 1909, President Theodore Roosevelt ordered the reservation included in a new Alamo National Forest, with land use to be subject to regulations promulgated by the Secretary of Agriculture. He did give the Mescalero people a 25-year grace period.

Three years later, President W. H. Taft removed that threat by restoring the Mescalero Reservation to its previous status, excluding it from the National Forest. Taft also cited a five percent tuberculosis rate among children in Mescalero boarding school as one argument for increased appropriations for Indian health care. All 91 able-bodied men and one woman farmed; all 91 and seven women owned livestock.

Another threat to reserved lands appeared immediately in the form of a bill introduced by New Mexico's new Senator A. B. Fall to make the reservation a national park. A rancher on the western edge of Mescalero Reservation, Fall persisted in introducing his bill for the next decade.

In 1913, Mescaleros took scores of wagons to Tularosa to transport 187 Apaches who had been interned at Ft. Sill, Oklahoma since 1894, to new reservation homes. Fewer than 10% were Mescaleros. The rest were Warm Springs and Chiricahua Apaches. All were survivors of the last hostiles interned by the U.S. in Florida in 1886, along with a number of loyal Apache Indian Scouts who had inexplicably been interned with the renegades whose capture they had just accomplished. Asa Daklugie explored the Mescalero Reservation for them in 1910 and obtained Mescalero approval for sharing their land. The federal government thus ended the anomaly of Indian "prisoners of war," many born at internment camps, after 28 years.

The Chiricahua Chato ("Flat Nose") had built himself a house at San Carlos, started raising horses and mules and farming 14 acres when he played a major role as a scout in Geronimo's final defeat. Gen. N. A. Miles placed him at the head of a delegation of Apaches sent to Washington to interview President Grover Cleveland and receive presidential medals from the Secretary of War. As Chato put it to General George Crook, whose life he saved, why was he given a medal to wear in the guard house? Expecting something good from the award, Chato found himself confined. Finally, he was able to enjoy the last years of his life in the relative freedom of Mescalero Reservation.

The in-gathering of the Mescalero Reservation population ended. A quarter century had passed since the last armed conflict between Apaches and U. S. citizens. The era of transition from frontier contacts to settled government in the Southwest drew to a close. New Mexico Territory gained admittance to the Union in 1912, placing the Mescalero Reservation within a state. The U. S. stood on the brink of the first World War. The time had come for Mescalero people to begin playing a larger role in setting policy for their reservation lands. Bureau of Indian Affairs high-handedness peaked in 1914 when it diverted grazing fee income from per capita payments to start a tribal herd.

Apprenticeship in Governance, 1918-1936. In

the final World War I year 1918, the people of Mescalero Reservation organized a Business Committee. A President who assumed the functions of head chief of everyone on the reservation headed the new body. Members of the Business Committee struggled against adverse odds. When it wanted to sell timber from the reservation over a 10-year period, Congress would not pass the necessary authorization. As a matter of fact, the Business Committee could not even spend the income whites paid for the privilege of exploiting reservation resources. The Congress had fallen into the habit of appropriating funds to pay Bureau of Indian Affairs employees and purchase their equipment from reservation income instead of the general tax revenues of the United States. Consequently, the Business Committee managed to make only relatively minor decisions. Its members served more of an apprenticeship in self government than they actually managed Mescalero affairs.

In 1919, former U. S. Army chaplain Albert Braun, O.F.M., took up the Roman Catholic missionary task at Mescalero. The doughty Franciscan raised cabbages and other vegetables to sell, having no other income. Nonetheless, he began in 1920 to build a stone church on a hill overlooking the village, aided by two laymen. The priest opened his own rock quarry, cut the stones, burned lime for mortar, felled timber, acted as mason, carpenter and sculptor. During

79

the New Deal, Rev. Braun served as a reserve officer chaplain to Civilian Conservation Corps camps in New Mexico, pouring his salary into his church construction project. Father Albert built up a congregation to worship in one of the most striking churches in the country. By 1940, he claimed 500 of the 700 people on the reservation as communicants. The Mescalero people turned to the faith their forefathers had explored more than a century earlier.

Initiative in U.S. Indian affairs still lay with Congress. In 1922, that body confirmed Mescalero title to the reservation. In 1924, Congress unilaterally pronounced all native Americans citizens of the republic. The Bureau that year started a five-year program to issue 10 sheep or 20 goats to any Mescalero reservation resident who would take part. Logging began on Elk and Silver Creeks the year before, and in 1926, the Bureau sold 175,000,000 feet of timber at $4 per thousand feet.

In general, Congressional control of tribal income stifled both economic development and emergence of real reservation self-determination. U. S. policy remained locked in an expectation that native Americans would continue to diminish until they disappeared. Policy makers appeared not to be aware that the historic population decline had ended and native Americans had begun to increase. Nor did they seem to appreciate the extent to which first Spanish and later Anglo-American individualism had weakened traditional family controls over young Mescaleros who refused to be bound by old customs. Mescalero eagerness for formal education accounted for much of this change. Students regularly overcrowded the local school. When capacity was 100 pupils in 1921-25, enrollment ran 106, 123, 139, 132 and 128. The Bureau rated capacity as 130 in 1926, and enrollment zoomed to 147.

On the other hand, boredom continued to be a prime fact of reservation life. Mescalero women remained addicted to gambling, playing the Mexican card games learned by their great-grandmothers when they should have been cooking dinner.

During the years after Stottler's strong-armed cultural change program, governmental prohibition of all public ceremonies except an annual girls' puberty rite established this as the most important surviving ritual. By 1932, only older men in conservative families could even remember the special training once given adolescent boys. Thus, Anglo-American repression exacted its cultural toll.

Indian New Deal, 1936-1946. Self-government on the Mescalero Reservation benefitted from the same encouragement during the New Deal reformation in Indian affairs that tribes generally received from Commissioner of Indian Affairs John Collier. Most fundamentally,

Congress in 1934 passed the Indian Reorganization Act. That law authorized reservation residents who voted to organize under the act to adopt written constitutions and representative forms of democratic reservation governance.

Mescalero delegates visited Santo Domingo Pueblo early in 1934 to hear the bill presented. After its passage, residents of the Mescalero Reservation voted in 1936 to adopt a constitution and federal charter making the Business Committee the effective government. The newly recognized reservation administration led by Victor Dolan promptly borrowed from a new federal revolving loan fund to finance building homes, many outside the agency town, and barns and poultry houses, purchasing implements and livestock from the former tribal herd now distributed to individual owners. By 1937, the new government had borrowed $163,000 and $242,000 by 1939 when 183 farm-units were finished.

The tribal constitution provided for a court to adjudicate cases not falling under federal jurisdiction. A Cattle Growers' Association managed reservation stock management for new owners. With solid backing from the Bureau, Mescalero cattlemen terminated all range leases to whites and began to graze Indian-owned cattle. Collier claimed that reservation cattle net income jumped from $18,000 to $101,000 during one three-year period, while crops increased eightfold. As Collier phrased it, the new tribal government gave the Mescaleros "their war-way once more, their chance for combat."

Inhabitants of this reservation may well have profited more from Collier's programs than those of any other jurisdiction. His program also involved shifting Mescalero students (among them young Wendell Chino, of whom more later) from boarding school to day schools with a revamped curriculum, expanded health service delivery, etc.

Commissioner Collier tried to appoint the most dynamic superintendents he could recruit to carry out his policies. His Mescalero superintendent from 1935 to 1938, E. R. McCray, embodied qualities Collier sought. He worked energetically to move people away from agency headquarters to live on arable land scattered about the reservation. The agency cut timber, sawed it, and put up four-room houses roofed with galvanized iron in yet another drive to move everyone out of tipis into Anglo-American-style homes, despite Mescalero ghost-fear and dwelling-abandonment after a death. Every reservation family had such a house by 1942. Business Committee Presidents Asa Daklugie (1938), Sam Kenoi (1939-40), Homer Yahnozha (1941) and Eric Tortilla led the tribe in borrowing $328,000 from the federal credit fund by 1944, more than any other reservation government.

By that time, the U. S. was at war and many Mescalero reservation people found wartime employment in other areas. These Apaches lived for the first time in Anglo-American towns and cities, earned high wages and glimpsed modern urban life. When the wartime boom ended, they returned to Mescalero Reservation with significantly altered outlooks. Led by Presidents Solon Sombrero (1943-44) and Fred Pellman (1945-46), the Business Committee had brought their homeland through the wartime crisis prepared for a new era.

Compensation and Termination, 1946-1965. Gyrations in U.S. Indian policy were never much more rapid than immediately following World War II. During the first post-war decade, the Mescalero people fared fairly well economically. Family income averaged $1,800 from 1946 to 1956. The Business Committee contributed to that well-being under Presidents Asa Daklugie (1947), Rufus Sago (1948-50), Wheeler Tissnolthtos (1951), Richard Magoosh (1952) and Wendell Chino (1953-55). A 1951 graduate of Western Theological Seminary, Holland, Michigan, Reformed Church minister Chino brought youth and new energy to the president's position.

In 1946, Congress passed an Indian Claims Commission Act allowing any Indian group that thought the U. S. had dealt unfairly with it to sue for damages. The Act established a special

84

Commission to hear complaints. Those who pushed the legislation through envisioned a final settling of moral accounts with mistreated native Americans.

Like over 300 other entities, the Mescalero Reservation government joined other Apaches in a suit against the U.S. The plaintiffs won, and the federal government in 1967 paid the Mescaleros $8,500,000. Some eighty percent was invested.

On the other hand, Commissioner Collier in 1944 returned to the theme of many an earlier Commissioner of Indian Affairs seeking money. He asked Congress for a larger budget so the Bureau could work itself out of a job. A new Commissioner and his associates in 1947 officially announced their goal of withdrawing federal services from Indians, issuing a preliminary classification of tribes in three groups estimated to be five, ten and 25 years away from being prepared for total cessation of federal services.

President H. S. Truman's Indian Affairs Commissioner initiated a program to encourage and subsidize the "relocation" of reservation residents to major cities to take up wage labor. Mescalero reservation population increased to 876 soon after World War II. Consequently, numerous families welcomed the program, and migrated to Los Angeles and San Francisco. All soon returned to the reservation, where

Mescalero village offers five churches, and in recent years a community center with swimming pool, bowling alley, game rooms, gymnasium, library and workshops, rifle clubs, boy and girl scout programs, etc.

At the beginning of the Eisenhower administration, Congress in 1953 made "termination" of federal services to Indians official policy with House Concurrent Resolution 108. That same year, Congress in Public Law 280 authorized states to assume both criminal and civil jurisdiction over reservations. The next year, Congress passed half a dozen bills terminating federal trusteeship over specific Indian lands. So much Bureau of Indian Affairs and Congressional attention focused upon these vanguard termination efforts that groups such as the Mescaleros were largely left to make their own way for several years.

President D. D. Eisenhower became appalled by the poor quality of health service delivery by the Bureau of Indian Affairs. One physician and one public health nurse operated a 40-bed hospital plus clinics on the Mescalero reservation, for example. Eisenhower in 1955 transferred health service responsibility to the U. S. Public Health Service, which could draft doctors to serve such remote facilities. Since then, USPHS has built a new 15-bed hospital at Mescalero village.

Several years of drought plus federal agricultural policies diminished Mescalero cattle income so drastically that the tribe lost $13,000 in 1956. Post-war prosperity ended.

The reservation government was already moving under President Wendell Chino to invest in reservation resource development to improve its economy. A tourist center at the summit of the 8,000 foot high pass on Highway 70 between Ruidoso and Mescalero village opened in September, 1956. Apache Summit's 12-unit motel, restaurants, craft sales shop, trailer park and picnic grounds in the pines represented a $200,000 tribal fund investment made under President Fred Pellman after a decade's debate.

During this period, young people began to seek college education so as to compete more effectively with non-Indians. By 1957, when Chino again led the Business Committee and furnished an outstanding example of the value of higher education, five pioneering students attended college.

The role of Mescalero women has changed under Anglo-American domination. Despite prevailing male chauvinism, Virginia Klinekole became President of the Business Committee in 1959-60, in a resurgence of Mescalero feminine leadership. Then Fred Pellman recaptured the office in 1961.

Mescaleros in the Great Society, 1963-1973. The Economic Opportunity Act Congress passed in 1964 at President L. B. Johnson's urging profoundly affected people on Mescalero Reservation. The tribal government had already staged its preview of Great Society programs beginning in 1963. Under President Wendell Chino, who succeeded Pellman in 1962, the Mescaleros borrowed $1,500,000 from the U. S. to purchase a ski run non-Indians had constructed on the north slope of Sierra Blanca, where a gondola tramway takes skiers to 11,400 feet. This enterprise 16 miles from Ruidoso turned into money-maker with over 300,000 annual visits.

After much preliminary work, a constitutional revision committee submitted to the people a new tribal constitution which they adopted by a vote of 190 to 103 on December 11, 1964. This document defined all residents of the reservation as members of the "Mescalero Apache Tribe," regardless of their historic tribal or band affiliations. It also recognized a bilateral descent system for tribal membership, providing that children of one Mescalero parent would become members of the tribe and shareholders in it.

The new constitution converted the Business Committee into a Tribal Council of eight members elected at large. Council members must be 25 years old when elected, must have resided on the reservation for at least six months prior to election and never have been convicted of a felony. They must meet at least quarterly. The revised basic governing document also established an Executive Department of tribal government headed by a President aided by a vice-president, secretary and treasurer. The President appoints the latter two officers; he and the vice-president are elected. After a special referendum rejected four-year terms, the constitutional revision committee provided two-year terms for all elected officials. Rev. Wendell Chino retained the Presidency, now that of the Mescalero Apache Tribe.

Mescalero Apache Tribal government under President Chino could move rapidly when Great Society programs started in 1965. The Mescaleros established a Head Start program to reduce the language handicap with which children entered school. The federal government opened a local Job Corps Center that year, one of only 10 on reservations. The tribal chief executive negotiated an agreement providing that the facility would revert to the tribe. In 1966, the Bureau of Sport Fisheries and Wildlife began to operate a trout hatchery producing 275,000 nine and 10-inch fish per year for reservation streams and beyond. The tribal government sold non-residents licenses to hunt, fish, and cut Christmas trees, thus augmenting its revenues. Almost any day, travelers on U. S. Highway 70 may see Apache youths catching plump Rainbow trout from the water-cress lined stream in front of the Mescalero Community Center.

Tribal President Chino obtained a Bank of New Mexico loan to start this large complex when most credit institutions would not lend to this reservation government. Opened in 1968, the Center not only provides offices for tribal executives and council-meeting chambers, but a cafeteria and recreational facilities.

The U. S. Department of Housing and Urban Development has erected low-rent housing units down-canyon from the main Mescalero village.

In 1970 under President R. M. Nixon, the federal government finally moved concretely to reduce traditional bureaucratic control of Mescaleros. It contracted with the tribe to have its personnel carry out many functions and services long performed by the Bureau of Indian Affairs.

That same year, Cannon Craft began to manufacture wooden shutters in the former Job Corps Center, thanks to the reversion clause in the original agreement. Absenteeism of Indian employees plus a mangement power struggle ended that source of jobs in the tribal industrial park the next year. Then Marvel Engineering took over the site in 1972 to produce industrial filters in large metal buildings reached by paved road through beautiful pine groves.

By that time, 19 youths attended college, so a small number of Mescaleros was acquiring skills to work at more demanding tasks than factory labor. The greatest investment commitment of

90

Photograph by Indian Tribal Series

TWO MESCALERO BOYS fishing for trout in the pond in front of the Community Center Building in Mescalero village.

the tribe lay in recreational development. In 1972, the Tribe paid each member-shareholder a dividend of approximately $400 from earnings by investments made with its Claim settlement, and launched its largest recreational development yet. After President Chino found a contractor to build a large earth-fill dam for one-sixth the cost estimated by the Bureau of Indian Affairs, the tribal government put the firm to work on the first stage of the Cieneguita Resort project. The dam will form a 100 to 140-acre lake, on the shores of which the tribe plans to build an 18-hole golf course and a tourist hotel, whose front windows will afford a magnificent view of the snowy peak of Sierra Blanca. Later, a dude ranch and hunting lodge are planned within the 30,000 acres set aside for this recreation complex to be reached by a new road from U. S. Highway 70. Situated on the first high, pine-clad mountains west of the major Texas cities, the reservation appears to be well located to profit from such recreational development.

Moreover, President Chino and his government plan a different type development near Silver Lake in the southern part of the reservation. Trailer pads and facilities will cater to visitors who prefer "roughing it" to the first-class tourist installation at Cieneguita.

Even though the Mescaleros leased their Summit Enterprise to a non-Indian in 1966, they have achieved impressive progress toward developing a reservation economy based on recreation as well as cattle grazing and timber harvesting, that will support a rapidly growing population at a standard of living comparable to that of non-Indians in southern New Mexico, even though that is inflated by defense spending. Besides paying a 1972 dividend on investments, the tribal government by 1973 employs 365 persons, making it the major source of wages for reservation families.

THE SECOND CENTURY

On May 29, 1973, nearly 2,000 members of the Mescalero Apache Tribe celebrate the centennial of the first presidential executive order reserving lands for Mescalero occupancy. There are now 460,563 such acres. As part of this celebration, Tribal President Wendell Chino plans to present an Indian peace medal to the President of the United States. President Chino decided that the occasion would be a fitting one for a first presentation of such a medal to the U. S. President by a native American tribal leader. He will thus reverse the custom of the first century of U. S. Indian policy when federal officials bestowed presidential medals upon Indian chiefs as symbols of peaceful allegiance. This portion of the Mescalero Reservation Centennial celebration symbolizes very well the attitude of calm and competent confidence with which members of the modern Mescalero Nation face their second century of reservation life and the Third Century of the United States of America. The Mescalero people today view themselves both as a still-sovereign native American entity and as U.S. good citizens, working toward ever more mutually rewarding cultural pluralism within their reserved area.

Today, the Mescalero people entertain no doubts about their ethnic survival. The grim decline of Mescalero population during the 19th and first two decades of the 20th Centuries ended, and reservation population increased to nearly 1,700 individuals in 1972. The youthful reservation population can be expected to increase more rapidly than the general U. S. population for many years in the future.

The centennial plans also symbolize the economic adjustments that the culturally adaptable Mescalero people have made. The professional economic raiders of 1850 have achieved a whole series of remarkable fundamental economic transformations under U. S. sovereignty that point to a bright future.

First, the Mescalero people, long conditioned to disdain manual labor and menial jobs such as herding, nonetheless learned to raise not only horses which brought a warrior prestige, but beginning in the 1880's cattle, and a decade later, sheep and goats. Some 130,000 acres of the reservation are classified as grazing land, and another 65,000 acres support only brush. Once

Photograph by Indian Tribal Series

MODERN HOUSING constructed with U. S. Department of Housing and Urban
Development assistance on the western edge of Mescalero, New Mexico.

free to choose, the Mescalero people specialized in raising cattle. Droughts in the 1950's taught the 42% of the people who own stock in Mescalero Cattle Growers, Inc., that their range cannot support on a permanent basis the 7,000 to 10,000 head it carries in good years. The Association must regard its 3,000-calf annual sales figure as a maximum and its present 6,000 Herefords as a sustained production-sized herd. The cattle industry has reached approximately maximum feasible development. Income will vary from year to year, depending on moisture conditions, stock improvement, possible alternative grazing animals, and market price, but only a portion of the population can live from its profits.

Settled life on Mescalero Reservation afforded an opportunity to raise irrigated crops. Some 3,600 acres are classed as arable, but some people consider only 300 farmable. Despite the tenacity with which the Plains Apaches carried on horticulture under Ute and Comanche attack between 1704 and 1725, relatively few Mescaleros farm today. Men who plowed fields as boys drive past weed-choked fields without a regret. There is an environmental limit on agricultural potential on this high-altitude reservation as well as the cultural limitation mostly derived from Spanish army-officer disdain for peasant farmers. The reservation simply suffers from a very short growing season.

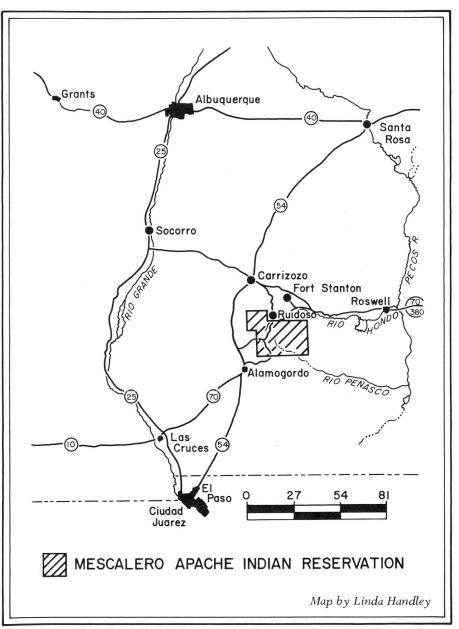

Grants

Albuquerque
(40)

(40)

Santa Rosa

(25)

(54)

Socorro

RIO GRANDE

Carrizozo

Fort Stanton

Roswell
(70)
(380)

Ruidoso

RIO HONDO

PECOS R.

Alamogordo

RIO PENASCO

(25)

(70)

Las Cruces
(10)

(54)

El Paso

Ciudad Juarez

0   27   54   81

MESCALERO APACHE INDIAN RESERVATION

Map by Linda Handley

MAP 4. The Mescalero Apache Indian Reservation today, showing highway access routes to this mountain winter and summer playground in the Southwest.

Under Bureau of Indian Affairs tutelage, people on the Mescalero Reservation learned a good deal about forestry. One-time aides now know how to scale timber, mark trees for cutting, and manage the forest, which occupies 261,300 reservation acres. Commercial logging entered an accelerated phase when dwarf mistletoe and a bark beetle threatened the pine and fir trees. In 1968 and 1971 fires killed more trees to be cleared and marketed. This accelerated cutting by private companies under contract will probably last until about 1980, along with extensive reforestation and reseeding. Then timber harvesting may have to be sharply curtailed so as to manage reservation timber resources on a sustained-yield basis. Timber income is cyclical, and will decline appreciably just when a large population increment comes onto the reservation job market.

The limited potential in each major economic activity that the Mescalero people first learned during the reservation century means that individuals must specialize to earn a future living. Some have become and will continue to be cowboys and range managers. Some will be foresters, some perhaps farmers. As recent developments demonstrate, some have become and will continue to be fish-hatchery workers. Some will be teachers specializing in primary bilingual education, because the Mescalero Reservation dialect of Athapascan is a flour-

98

Photograph by Indian Tribal Series

MESCALERO APACHE TRIBE PRESIDENT WENDELL CHINO points across what will soon be an artificial lake impounded by the earth-fill dam behind him toward the site of the Tribe's planned resort hotel. He stands on a ridge between what will be two arms of the lake, near the first hole of the planned 18-hole golf course.

ishing first language in the reservation home, and pupils must learn English as a second language.

Beginning in an exploratory way with Summit Enterprise and decisively with the Sierra Blanca Ski Enterprise, the reservation government invested in recreational facilities opening up a wide range of new occupations. These service occupations require tourist customers, as did traditional basket-making for cash sale. They differ from earlier Mescalero occupations in that they serve non-Indians who come onto the reservation to share the beauty of these forested mountains and their cool streams. So Mescaleros are becoming game wardens and managers, guides, hotel clerks, electricians, plumbers, carpenters, maids and all the kinds of workers needed to operate a large-scale recreation industry. They will be mechanics, drivers and gasoline-station attendants to serve 10,000,000 people who live within one day's drive.

Among necessary occupations are those of bookkeeper, accountant, economist, market researcher, clerk, stenographer, public-relations worker, nurse, photographer, policeman and policy maker. The labor force available on the reservation already numbers over 600. Of key importance to the future of the Mescalero people will be the quality of leadership in reservation governance. Construction of the large new headquarters at the edge of town in 1968 evidenced the emergence of a full-scale bureaucracy that can but increase in size and complexity in future.

Just what course its expansion may take is impossible to predict. About the only safe prediction about reservation politics is that they cannot be predicted. President Chino could be re-elected to numberless additional terms, or he could be defeated at the next election. Clearly, however, college-educated Mescaleros like this first full-time paid President will be in great demand in tribal government, the recreation industry, and timber and cattle management. As evidence of past tribal government concern for the future is a $600,000 investment of Claims-payment funds to produce income to finance college scholarships for Mescalero students who attend such institutions of higher learning as New Mexico State University at Las Cruces, Eastern New Mexico University at Portales, and the University of New Mexico in Albuquerque. The number of college graduates will increase, so there will come a time during the second reservation century when the members of the reservation governing council as well as its president will be highly educated individuals.

Whether they will be ordained Christian ministers like President Chino, or devout native religionists, who can say? The frequency of native ceremonies appears to have declined in recent years, yet pan-Indian religious movements may spark a Mescalero religious revival at any time. For a number of years, Mescalero families with daughters ready for puberty ceremonies have scheduled these on July 4th, as part of a reservation Ceremonial that includes dances and a rodeo. This helps attract tourists, so secularization of the women's puberty rite appears sure to continue. Yet the very economic motivation for holding the rite on the Ceremonial date will also probably assure its survival, albeit in less sacred form than in former times.

Among Christians, denominational competition will go on. Already the Assembly of God, Baptists and Church of Jesus Christ of Latter Day Saints claim a third of the reservation population, the Reformed Church about a third, and the Roman Catholic Church a third. Once pioneer missionaries demonstrated Mescaleros could be converted to Christianity, interdenominational rivalry became inevitable.

The Mescalero people will increasingly control the alcoholic beverages with which Spanish colonial officials tried to exterminate them. Led by a teetotaler President, they hold state liquor licenses to sell alcoholic beverages to their customers at Apache Summit and Sierra Blanca Ski Area. A referendum vote legalized liquor sales on the reservation by a five to one margin. A tribal lounge already serves to keep serious drinkers off the highways, thus sharply diminishing fatal highway accidents formerly associated with quests for off-reservation sources of modern relatives of *tulapai.*

Technologically, the Mescalero of the future will differ little from neighboring non-Indians. Already the Mescalero people wear clothing purchased in the same stores as other New Mexicans, drive Ford, Oldsmobile and Lincoln automobiles, live in frame and brick homes with indoor kitchens and plumbing. The tribe provides domestic water, Otero County REA electricity, and private companies butane fuel. With V. E. Stottler only a bitter memory, a few Mescaleros now enjoy circulating air fireplaces and picture windows, and more will in the future.

The proud Mescalero people will not brook Stottler-style dictation from white authorities this next century!

SUGGESTED READINGS

A huge historical literature about the Mescalero people is largely not accessible to the ordinary reader. Most of the best anthropoligical studies are buried in technical journals. A few fine historical studies are readily purchased or can be consulted in major libraries.

CREMONY, JOHN C. *Life Among the Apaches.* San Francisco: A. Roman & Co. (1951 reprint by Arizona Silhouettes, Tucson), 1868.

Fascinating chapters about Mescaleros in defeat by a California Volunteer officer who established a unique relationship with them at Ft. Sumner.

HOIJER, HARRY. *Chiricahua and Mescalero Texts.* Chicago: University of Chicago Press, 1938.

Technical linguistics publication, but provides significant folklore texts.

MOORHEAD, MAX L. *The Apache Frontier: Jacobo Ugarte and Spanish-Indian Relations in Northern New Spain, 1769-1791.* Norman: University of Oklahoma Press, 1968.

This history of one colonial officer offers more information about Mescaleros on Spain's frontier than any other single work.

SONNICHSEN, C. L. *The Mescalero Apaches.* Norman: University of Oklahoma Press, 1973 second revised edition.

The standard history of the Mescalero people, more detailed than this book on the century of reservation life and U.S.–Mescalero conflict, but thinner on Spanish-Mescalero interaction. Highly recommended.

Actual Size

THE MINTAGE of the massive Mescalero Apache Peace Medals was limited to 350 pieces, and represent an historical first, as referred to on page 93.

THE AUTHOR

HENRY F. DOBYNS, Professor of Anthropology at Prescott College, chaired the Department of Anthropology at the University of Kentucky from 1966 to 1970. Earlier he was Lecturer and Senior Research Associate in the Cornell University Department of Anthropology, where he coordinated the Comparative Studies of Cultural Change and Andean Indian Community Research-and-Development Program in Ecuador, Peru, and Bolivia. Born in Tucson, Arizona, Dobyns received the B.A. and M.A. degrees from the University of Arizona, and the Ph.D. degree from Cornell University. A researcher for the Hualapai, Havasupai, Papago and Pima tribes in Arizona, Dobyns analyzed the documentary history of Lipan and Mescalero Apaches with Dr. Morris E. Opler, the main anthropological expert on Apachean culture.

Dobyns' writing for Indian Tribal Series is familiar to its readers. With Paul L. Doughty and Harold D. Lasswell, he edited *Peasants, Power, and Applied Social Change: Vicos as a Model,* recording how Cornell University anthropologists helped native American serfs on a highland Peruvian hacienda become prosperous and self-governing.

106